The Man Behind the Smile

Tony Blair and the Politics of Perversion

First of all, you must learn the constitution of man and the modifications which it has undergone, for originally it was different from what it is now. In the first place there were three sexes, not, as with us, two, male and female; the third partook of the nature of both the others and has vanished, though its name survives. The hermaphrodite was a distinct sex in form as well as in name, with the characteristics of both male and female, but now the name alone remains, and that solely as a term of abuse ... Each of us then is the mere broken tally of a man, the result of a bisection which has reduced us to a condition like that of a flatfish, and each of us is perpetually in search of a corresponding tally.

Plato's Symposium

Also by Leo Abse and published by Robson Books

Wotan, My Enemy

The Man Behind the Smile

Tony Blair and the Politics of Perversion

LEO ABSE

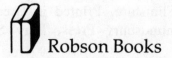

Robson Books

First published in Great Britain in 1996 by
Robson Books Ltd, Bolsover House, 5–6
Clipstone Street, London W1P 8LE

British Library Cataloguing in Publication Data
A catalogue record for this title is available from
the British Library

ISBN 1 86105 078 X

'An Apology' by Fleur Adcock is reproduced by
permission of the author.

Photoset in North Wales by Derek Doyle &
Associates, Mold, Flintshire. Printed in Great
Britain by St Edmundsbury Press, Bury St
Edmunds, Suffolk.

To Marjorie in memoriam

and to Tobias, Bathsheba and Giuseppe

Contents

Acknowledgements   ix

John Smith: The Lost Leader   1

Charisma I: Hugh Gaitskell   13

Charisma II: Aneurin Bevan   27

Androgynous Politics: Tony Blair   51
    Warning: You Are Entering a Conflict-Free Zone   53
    Exhibitionism: Do I Exist?   66
    The Outsiders: Leo and Tony   78
    Disavowals   87
    Traumatic Families   106
    Fellow-Feeling of the Unsound   126
    Rock   130
    Blair's Palingenetic Myth   144
    The Hermaphrodite and the Androgynous:
      The Distinction   164
    Politics of Perversion   169
    A Dire Misfit   186
    A Rum Entourage   199
    Deadwood   208

Bibliography   216

Index   221

Acknowledgements

Responsibility for the contents and blemishes of this book is solely mine. But responsibility for the book having been written must be shared by my friend Geoffrey Goodman, broadcaster and one-time industrial editor of the Mirror group, whose sustained incitements ensured this work was commenced and completed.

I am indebted to my psychoanalyst brother, Dr Wilfred Abse, Emeritus Professor of Psychiatry of the University of Virginia, whose publications in the 1960s first brought to my attention the relationship between charismatic political leadership and hermaphroditism, the starting-point of this polemical essay. To Brett Kahr, biographer and senior lecturer in psychotherapy at Regent's College, I also owe particular thanks for the assistance he generously gave me when wrestling with the chapter 'The politics of perversion'.

I am grateful to my historian son, Dr Tobias Abse, and my fellow-solicitor Andrew Stephenson of Messrs Peter Carter-Ruck & Partners, who both read the penultimate draft of the book and who have protected me from some of my extravagances.

I am in considerable debt to Frances Hawkins, my indefatigable amanuensis who by her constant vigilation, her critical appraisements, and her preliminary editing, has played an important part in the shaping of this book.

I am grateful to the Institute of Psycho-Analysis for access to their library, and to librarian Jill Duncan who has been unfailingly helpful.

My publisher, Jeremy Robson, and my editor, Louise Dixon, to my good fortune, continue, with exquisite tact, to handle an irascible old man.

And, once again, I would wish to acknowledge my indebtedness to the Torfaen Labour Party and the electors of the Eastern Valley of Gwent who gave me the opportunity for thirty years to participate at Westminster in the strange life of the children of the Mother and Father of Parliaments.

This book was written in difficult circumstances during a period when I lost my wife. I would wish to record my thanks to Dr Stephen Hirst, and to Professors Humphrey Hodgson and James Scott, Mr Witold Kmiot and Debbie Johnson of the Hammersmith Hospital, all of whom, by their dedication, so sustained my family.

John Smith:

The Lost Leader

On 12 May 1994 the Leader of Her Majesty's Opposition, the Right Honourable John Smith, lost his gamble. A heart attack he had endured had made him aware of his vulnerability, but he was not content to amble along as a respected backwoods Edinburgh lawyer. His ambition was greater, as was his capacity; he took the fateful risk, and plunged back into politics. When death cruelly mocked his daring, the whole nation mourned. The British Labour movement stood bereft. In the Commons John Smith's peers huddled together, comforting each other in their desolation, and would not engage in a bitter fratricidal struggle for the succession; the precepts of their lost leader governed them. They believed, as the nation believed, that a good man had been taken from them; and that perception was correct, for there was a singular lack of dissimulation in John Smith. Unlike most politicians, his public image and his private life were wholly congruent.

I encountered him, and learned of him, during the bitter devolution debates that in 1978 and 1979 took place in and out of Parliament when, yielding to aggressive nationalist clamour, a weak Labour government, struggling to remain in power with a precarious majority that could be endangered by nationalist MPs, sought to impose upon Wales and Scotland a form of government to which Wales was overwhelmingly hostile, and one to which many in Scotland were indifferent. In the Labour

3

Party devolution issues, as now again in 1996, can arouse rare political passions. John Smith, on the front bench, was one of the two main government spokesmen attempting to steer through a devolution Bill, one to which I was wholly opposed. In a parliamentary ploy, I sponsored, with considerable support, what is termed a 'reasoned amendment' to the Bill, and thus succeeded in wresting from the government, as a precondition to implementation of the devolution proposals, that first they had to be approved by way of a referendum by the electorate of Wales and Scotland. It was during that referendum campaign that I came into direct conflict with John Smith; and even as with one's enemies we often learn to understand them more than those we love, for love can be blind, so in political disputes, we sometimes can measure opponents more objectively than allies. I did not find John Smith wanting.

The catalyst which brought me nearer to the man was a televised Oxford Union debate when he, together with Emlyn Hooson, now a Liberal peer, put the case for devolution and I, together with Leon Brittan, opposed the motion. Although I suspect, and hope, the Oxford Union is altered and that the undergraduates now are less politically precocious and less precious, in the 1970s it was an anachronism; the youngsters rôle-played *Brideshead Revisited* parts, Edwardian postures were affected, carefully prepared impromptu interventions were *de rigueur*, and a painfully self-conscious style and strained wit gained disproportionate approval. I had often been invited to speak at the Oxford and Cambridge Unions and, although I had been much disconcerted on my first attendance by the responses, I was familiar with their absurd and highly mannered nonsense and had long since made the necessary adjustment, had accepted the prevailing idiom, and consequently many times enjoyed a good dinner and an evening out away from the tedium of the Commons. But this devolution debate was not fun; it was for real. The referendum polling date was near – St David's Day 1979 – and a substantial section of the electorate, certainly in Wales, was viewing the programme; it was not possible, however, simply to use the occasion to speak over the heads of the undergraduates to the voters; reverberations coming from within the audience would resound through the screen and a negative or positive response by the youngsters could play a part in influencing the votes of the viewers. It was necessary, therefore, to tailor one's contribution in the short time available to two disparate groups; and laughter and high seriousness had to be conjoined.

I was comfortable in my contribution, and all went very well; but the debate for the pro-devolutionists was a disaster. John Smith was disadvantaged by his professional legal training, and even more by a speaking style developed during his arduous student debates at Glasgow University, traditionally conducted with an earnestness and intensity frowned upon in the Oxford Union, where frivolity and irony were overvalued. Thus ill-equipped, Smith could not adapt, and although his earnest, heavy-handed, studiously prepared piece would have passed well enough in a court or in Glasgow, coming from the ambience of the Union it was a catastrophe; and, of course, he possessed the sensibility, even before he completed his speech, to know that he had failed.

The following morning we did not travel back to London together and for a while he avoided me in the lobbies of Westminster. But when, many months later, in an important Commons debate he made a devastating attack upon the Tories, who wilted as, with fact and logic, he assailed them, I congratulated him; he was half embarrassed by my praise and immediately ruefully recalled his dissonant Oxford speech. But, more revealingly, he began criticising the speech I was deservedly praising; he commenced categorising its omissions and its flaws, all of which in fact were, at most, peccadilloes. He was not seeking from me disclaimers, reassurances that they were of no importance; on the contrary, he wanted corroboration from me that his self-criticisms were totally valid.

This was unusual behaviour. Among MPs after a debate there is only too often a sickening display of hypocritical mutual

congratulation between participants, each telling the other how
splendidly he had performed; but John Smith wanted no such
massaging. And, because he knew I would be cruelly objective, I
was to find that from time to time, after a speech, he would
sometimes approach me shyly, not asking but waiting for my
assessment. Always, however, no matter how good I said his
content and presentation had been, still he insisted on their
inadequacy; becoming aware of the pattern, I recall once telling
him to cease punishing himself, but it was to no avail. The
perfectionist was in the grip of a malady, a condition described
by the French poet Mallarmé as the 'malady of the ideal'. The
coronary he was to suffer was not the cause of his death; that
thrombosis was but a symptom of that fateful malady.

His affliction was his compulsive search for the ideal; and that
ideal had been set for him by his card-carrying Labour Party
headmaster father, whose school he had attended. There he was
expected to get it right even when other children were out of
their depths: 'It was always "Why weren't you top of the class?"
In the end it was easier just to be top of the class,' he once said.
And always his father's injunction governed him as he walked
up, as was his wont, to the top of mountains or when he sought
perfection in the attainments of himself and in himself. His quest
for perfection brought many benefits for the Labour Party as the
shoddy glitz and superficiality of the Kinnock era gave way to
John Smith's painstaking insistence upon well-thought-out
policies and careful political stratagems informed by high
standards and moral values. To some at the top of his party, this
was an unwelcome approach. There are politicians for whom
stillness is death and who, to survive, must forever live in a
frenzy of excitement. They cannot tolerate delay and, presenting
their inchoate notions in language as vague as their content,
inflict upon us premature and faulty decision-making; they insist
tomorrow is today and anyone who challenges their novel
calendar is dubbed a 'yesterday man'. John Smith, in private
Labour political circles, was so labelled by the self-styled
modernisers surrounding Tony Blair, who peddled the tale that

the resistant Smith was stubborn, arrogant and impervious to change.

That tension should have arisen between Smith and Blair was predictable; the one had genuine and profound roots in community, in the little Scottish fishing village where he had lived out his childhood, and knew and understood the value of continuity, and indeed had revelled in writing a history of his own settled family from the eighteenth century onwards; the other was essentially a gypsy, the son of a man who held strong but ever vacillating political views, sometimes communist, sometimes High Tory, as he wandered, dragging his family with him even to the Antipodes, forever burdened with the irrational guilt of the illegitimate and forever concealing his ambiguous lineage from his own family. Smith was a man with roots; Blair is rootless. That their attitudes to the traditions of the Labour Party should have differed was a consequence; the one respected those traditions, the other irreverently dismissed them.

Smith felt, as a country village lad with the sea in his ears, 'the very pulse of the machine' and loathed disruption in the elemental, in the determined rivens within life. Abortion repelled him and, unlike the majority of his party, he consistently voted against those seeking to relax the existing laws. His abhorrence was principled; it gave him no political advantage. He represented a constituency with only a small number of Roman Catholics; he was certainly not yielding to lobby pressures. Despite all my persuasions, he supported Enoch Powell's 1985 Bill which would have criminalised research on embryos. In vain did I plead with Smith to desist in his support, telling him that abortion ended life but that *in vitro* fertilisation created life and gave the infertile the boon of parenthood. He was unconvinced and voted against my amendments to Powell's Bill. In the end I was able to wreck that Bill only by filibustering, making hours-long speeches that sabotaged Powell's parliamentary timetable.

But such stances by Smith gave overzealous Blairites full opportunity to misrepresent him as rigidly conservative, lacking the will to make the necessary changes in party and national policies. That, however, was not the appraisement made by a large section of the public. Taking another view, many increasingly responded to one whom they saw as making a serious effort to meet the nation's problems, and one who, at last, possessed *gravitas*; it was unexciting politics but it was honest and deserved respect. The private man, refusing to be precipitate and striving overconscientiously to remove blemishes from all the policies he hoped one day to implement, was paying a heavy price for the approval which he was slowly but increasingly gaining from the public; for in his pursuit of such policies he was severely handicapped, weighed down with guilt as he was that, by his honest presentation of the tax implications of Labour's policies during the 1992 General Election, he had let himself and his party down, and had contributed to the subsequent defeat. He felt he had not lived up to the standards he had set himself as a political strategist.

The mood that scorched John Smith, his recurring sense of dissatisfaction with himself however great his actual achievement, is recognisably a theme running through Freud's earliest papers and which continued into his last work. Freud regarded dissatisfaction as endemic to the human condition: 'There is always something lacking for complete ... satisfaction; *en attendant toujours quelque chose qui ne venait point* [always waiting for something which never comes].' Total contentment is denied to mankind; at the most, the happiness that comes from satisfaction of needs 'is from its nature only possible as an episodic phenomenon'. This disposition, Freud believed, was genetically determined and, reductively, he commented: 'However strange it may sound we must reckon with the possibility that something in the nature of the sexual instinct is unfavourable to the realisation of complete satisfaction.' Those who impose upon themselves excessively high ideals and targets in their restless search for fulfilment are denying biology; they are attempting to abolish the distance between their ego and their ego-ideal, but no matter how much they strain themselves, they are in danger of plunging fatally into what is an unbridgeable ravine. And so, to our loss, it happened to John Smith.

According to opinion polls taken in the months before his death, 72 per cent of the electorate believed 'he looked to be like a man with high moral standards and with the air of a family doctor or bank manager'. Nevertheless, by March 1994 the MORI pollsters were still able to interpret their statistics to disparage John Smith. They reported: 'John Smith has failed to inspire the voters; his rating remains evenly balanced with 38 per cent of the public in favour and against.' John Smith, however, patiently fought on and when he died Labour was reported to have a lead over the Tories of 21 per cent. After John Smith's death, believing such a lead was unsustainable – certainly until some new leadership had over time established itself – the Labour Party displayed scrupulous and rare political tact. Those with judgement and more intimate knowledge of the capacities of the possible contenders were aware that Robin Cook, with his past commitment to the Labour movement, his integrity, extraordinarily high intelligence and piercing debating skills, was best fitted for the challenging task; but he, selflessly, disqualified himself. A public debauched by meretricious television, conditioned to demand the photogenic, to mistake image for content, would probably have ill received such a leader. And another possible contender of ability, Gordon Brown, for personal as much as political reasons, chose not to be a contestant. With the field thus limited, Blair was poised to be a front-runner; and, although Labour Party activists were sceptical and 47 per cent of the party members did not vote for this untried, untested man, the new method of election of a Labour leader, founded on the one man one vote principle and with many more than ever before participating, gave the crown to Blair.

And then came the astonishing consequence. By a political chemistry unable to be adequately analysed by all the confounded conventional commentators, the unknown Blair, within weeks, achieved a result which all the painstaking work of John Smith had failed to bring about; and it occurred despite the polls telling us that at that time an increased optimism about the economic outlook was abroad. While in May 1994, in answer to the question who will make the best prime minister, 31 per cent declared for John Smith, in August 1994, 45 per cent declared for Blair. The Gallup polls showed that Labour commanded more widespread support than any party in Gallup's 57-year history and the Labour lead over the Conservatives was, by a wide margin, the largest either of the major parties had ever enjoyed over the other. Anthony King presented the Gallup poll figures and emphasised: 'Far more voters declare that Blair would make the best prime minister than ever thought that of John Smith, though his standing was high.' By the end of August the MORI poll revealed not only that the election of Blair as leader had resulted in a shift of middle-class and southern voters behind the Labour Party but also that a big shift in voting intentions had taken place among women throughout the country.

Some of the perplexed political commentators sought to dismiss this sea change in public opinion as a temporary infatuation; the 'honeymoon' period would soon be over. A very few others, more insightful, hazarded a guess that, as had occurred in other European countries – such as Italy, where the death of the communist leader Berlinguer had resulted in the subsequent gain of political support by his party – the reparative guilt which could bring about such occurrences would fade once the mourning period for John Smith was over. Such prognostications proved spurious; time has shown that the phenomenon of Blair cannot be so explained. And since the divisions and sleaze of the government, although since exacerbated, were in place at John Smith's death, Blair's sudden and immediate leap into electoral popularity cannot be attributed to Tory follies. Even if the polls showed, by the summer of 1996, that among some who had initially rallied to him there was now more grudging support, still Blair, in contrast to Major, was overwhelmingly regarded as being a stronger leader, a man with better ideas and more in touch with ordinary people.

What then has been the magic at work that has enabled an almost unknown political figure to gain, and substantially sustain, such popularity? Has a charismatic leader emerged? We have had our Thatcher but we are more accustomed to noting charismatic leadership in other lands: Gandhi in India, Hitler in Germany, Mandela in South Africa. We live in a more temperate political climate, inhospitable to exotics. Nevertheless, in my political lifetime I have witnessed two leaders in the Labour movement, Hugh Gaitskell and Aneurin Bevan, possessed of a charisma which hosts of followers found irresistible. Is Blair of a similar order, and are the resonances he has teased out of a large section of the electorate attributable to the same elusive qualities, the same bewildering fugitive traits, which enabled Gaitskell and Bevan to cast their spells? If, as seems increasingly likely, Blair becomes prime minister of Britain, will his triumph be primarily due then to an ineluctable factor, and in attempting to capture and anatomise it, are we chasing a will-o'-the-wisp? 'There are,' Henri Peyre once wrote, 'three subjects on which no wise man should ever attempt to write: love, genius and leadership. Of the three, the last is the most mysterious and the most unpredictably and capriciously feminine.' The advice of the famed French cultural critic may be sage, but fools sometimes successfully step in where wise men fear to tread.

Charisma I:

Hugh Gaitskell

The term 'charisma' was once used to describe the endowment of a leader blest or chosen by the gods. It was the quality and circumstance which we find described by the unknown founding father of Western history, long before Herodotus, in the Book of Samuel, where we learn of the emergence of a man upon whom the spirit of the Lord had fallen, King David – the magic poet-warrior, lover of Bathsheba and of Jonathan, the man 'wise in speech and handsome', whom Christianity claims as the progenitor of Christ. The term in its original but not modern sense lingers on in the Anglican Renewal services of the Church of England, in the Nonconformist Elim Pentecostal Church and among the self-declared charismatics who, although not necessarily possessing charisma, believed they were chosen by God and have sometimes, as political leaders, played a significant historical rôle in the last century: the demagogic and neurotic Theodor Herzl, whose shadow still falls across democratic Israel, was possessed of messianic delusions prompted by a dream that God had chosen him to lead his people; and the United States' President Nixon, all of whose siblings were stricken fatally with tuberculosis, believed himself to have been selected by divine intervention. Today, however, shoddy journalists have debased the term in both its original and its modern sense; promiscuously they bestow the rare attribute upon media 'celebrities'. Such glib labelling will certainly not enable us to divine the constituents of the thaumatological qualities attributed to Tony Blair by many of his supporters and by not a few of his opponents.

If, then, we are to be successful in our quest, using as our clinical material the past Labour leaders Gaitskell and Bevan, who enthralled so many, we must be armed with the findings of the two modern disciplines, political sociology and psycho-analysis, which have explored the phenomenon of charismatic leadership. To metabolise those findings, and then to ask whether, when applied to Blair, they validate or negate the claim that he is possessed of such leadership, may be a tough intellectual exercise, but it is an inescapable one; it may lead us into strange byways, but I do not believe that there is any other way to decode the vocabulary and grammar of the unspoken tongue of charisma, and consequently to learn whether Blair is genuinely in command of that outlandish language.

In political sociology we find the term charisma is austerely employed; its definition was provided by Max Weber, one of the founders of modern sociology, and the passing of the years has in no way subverted his description of the phenomenon. Max Weber saw charisma, in its relation to political power, as an extraordinary quality possessed by a person thought to give him a unique magical power. The man who possesses genuine charisma exercises a domination different from legal and traditional domination, for his power of command is extra-ordinary. Legal and traditional domination can become quasi-permanent structures that provide for everyday com-munity life. But in changing times, such structures may become ill-adapted to the satisfaction of community needs. Weber believed, therefore, that in times of difficulties the 'natural' leader may be neither the usual official nor the master whose authority is based on the sanctity of tradition, but rather the man who is believed to possess extraordinary gifts of body and mind.

From this sociological point of view, such leaders may be prophets or heroes, magicians or demagogues; but as long as they dominate by virtue of charisma, the relationship of leader and followers is of the same general type. For better or worse, charismatic leadership is especially in demand in times of war and its increased incidence in such seasons often carries revolutionary implications incompatible with traditional authority. On the other hand, the appeal of charisma may also be used to support traditional authority and, for example, to oppose necessary adaptational change.

Weber maintained that charismatic leadership of an extreme type occurs frequently in emergencies and is then associated with a collective excitement in which masses of people surrender themselves to an 'heroic' leader. The leader dominates by virtue of a quality inaccessible to others and incompatible with the rules of thought and action that may govern everyday life. The people can then turn away from established rules and submit to the unprecedented order that the leader proclaims. In this way, an inward reorganisation of outlook and experience of themselves can be effected by masses of people. Such processes of inner disorganisation, already begun in the period of stress, succeeded by reorganisation, are in contrast with the more superficial adaptations that occur apart from charismatic leadership – when people adapt themselves to a major change in legal rules without at the same time internalising the ideas and feelings behind it. Clearly charismatic leadership involves a high degree of commitment on the part of the followers, well beyond that involved in other types of domination.

To Max Weber's concepts, based on his empirical and historical studies, some psychoanalysts insist on adding an additional qualification before they are prepared to label a leader as genuinely charismatic. Since a charismatic leader, they affirm, needs his followers as much as the actor needs his audience, such a leader will have the capacity, in this interdependence, to maintain the cohesion of his group of followers by keeping aggressiveness in suspense and diverting it towards out-groups. Gandhi and Mandela, as charismatic leaders, had their out-groups grimly provided, the one in British imperialists, the other in the South African whites; and Hitler created his own out-group in the Jews. Within our domestic scene, in the Labour

Party, Gaitskell and Bevan bound their followers together by fiercely attacking, with considerable verve, not only Tories, but also opponents within their own party; and because they were engaged in a civil war, each leader targeting the same people within the Labour Party, seeking to enlist them to their own group, the battle, by British political standards, was a bloody one.

By the time, as a result of a 1958 by-election, I entered Parliament, Bevan had conceded defeat; but although he had deserted his own cause, the spell he had cast remained in place, and his followers held firmly to their belief in unilateral disarmament. The party's failure to come to terms with the ultimate violence, the hydrogen bomb, was tearing it asunder. The very minute I entered the Chamber to be sworn in as a new member, I was made depressingly aware by Gaitskell that I had gained entry into a battleground, not a united parliamentary party. Flanked by two South Wales colleagues, one of whom was my friend George Thomas, later Viscount Tonypandy, I had made my obeisance, moving from the bar of the House at slow pace and bowing three times to the Speaker. Then, after being sworn in before an observing House and receiving a kindly welcome from the Speaker, I moved, as I had been instructed by the attending Whips, behind the Speaker's chair. By convention, the Leader of the Party then leaves the Opposition front bench and also stands behind the Speaker's chair to greet the newly arrived member. Gaitskell's greeting was a frigid one; he gave me a wan smile, a less than half-hearted handshake, and a few perfunctory muttered words too strangled even to be heard. I felt his antagonism.

Gaitskell's reaction brought home to me the seriousness with which he took my identification with the Campaign for Nuclear Disarmament in Wales, which had caused the press to label me as an anti-Gaitskellite. A few years earlier, as the chairman of the Cardiff City parties I had received Gaitskell on his visits to the principality and, with the local MP, Jim Callaghan, had dined him and his wife. Callaghan always wanted me to act as host since he has a permanently stiff elbow joint which prevents him from reaching to his pocket and he knew I would pick up the restaurant bill. On such occasions Gaitskell had vainly endeavoured to beguile me, hoping to convince me of the error of my ways; but Callaghan, after I had led his constituency to reprimand him for his presumptuous endeavour to expel Bevan from the Labour Party – the action of a gnat seeking to drive an elephant from his stamping grounds – knew better than to make the attempt.

However, Gaitskell's vexation that I had gained entry to the Commons had a particular origin: it had frustrated a ploy played by Gaitskell and Callaghan to bring into the House a powerful steel union boss who was a strong Gaitskell supporter. Gaitskell promoted the elevation of my undistinguished predecessor to the Lords and so created a vacancy in the safe seat of Pontypool, then regarded as a steel constituency; and with a little manipulation they believed the local party could be persuaded to adopt their favourite. Events proved otherwise. Welsh political life is ever convoluted, and its zest and vitality are to be found in the conspiracies and stealth which must precede every decision; nothing could be less tolerable than a prosaic and predictable straightforward result. Once it was known by the initiates that the Gaitskellite-dominated National Executive of the Labour Party was manoeuvring to have a compliant MP representing the constituency, the fate of the steel boss was sealed. The local party, despite pressures, stubbornly refused even to place him on their short list, and the success of those supporting my candidature was thus assured. It was not surprising to me, therefore, that Gaitskell, at Westminster, received me with less than enthusiasm.

Although I found Gaitskell antipathetic, there is no doubt that he fascinated many people. When I was with him I was always aware in particular of his caressing voice, which was extraordinarily seductive. In most other species it is the male which possesses the bodily characteristics which are the biological bases of charm used in the service of sexual union. But even if man is one of what Darwin called the anomalous cases, in which there has been an almost complete transfer of secondary orientation to the female, the male is not left totally bereft – and Gaitskell could certainly bewitch the birds in the trees; for not only men but women too would quickly fall under his spell. He possessed at least some of the qualities of a genuinely charismatic leader, for the charm which is the main asset of a charismatic leader, at once both weapon and armour, is one which conveys not only his magic power but also his delicate need for love and protection, and such protection was passionately offered Gaitskell by what the political commentators of the time rightly described as his praetorian guard.

But it was more than my political stances that created the gulf between us. His whole political culture and, in particular, the style of leadership which grew out of that culture were alien to me. In the year I was elected, the Wykehamist, with an arrogance unsuccessfully masked in an excruciating and sickly display of saintliness, patronisingly declared: 'We, as middle-class socialists, have got to have a profound humility. Though it's a funny way of putting it, we've got to know that we lead them because they can't do it without us, with our abilities, and yet we must feel humble to working people.'

Fortunately for me, I came from South Wales, where, in my youth, outside a small band in Cardiff, there was, in effect, no middle class. The coal-owners, the capitalists, the big land-owners, the steel magnates, were all absentee landlords. It is true that in the valleys of South Wales there would be a clustering together of the local doctor, the mines manager, the solicitor, the forge manager and some comfortably off shopkeepers who, since no local aristocracy existed, would play-act as lords and ladies; but these members of the *petit bourgeoisie* dissociated themselves completely from the overwhelmingly solid proletarian majority which threateningly surrounded them. They certainly provided no leadership or expertise to the workers.

And those workers, without the 'abilities' of Wykehamists, and doing without middle-class mentors, created a trade union and labour movement possessed of a rare political sophistication. It was within that working-class culture that I had learned my political craft. I had therefore been tutored in irreverence, sceptical of the largesse bestowed by middle-class reformers; their contributions were not sacramental, and were not necessarily part of my canon. I was already alerted. I approved, but did not need, the warning given by Nye Bevan when, in 1938, he mocked the hauteur of reforming experts:

> The people are excluded from forming judgement on various matters of public interest on the ground that expert knowledge is required, and that of course the people cannot possess ... The debunking of the expert is an important stage in the history of democratic communities because democracy involves the assertion of the common against the special interest ... The first weapon in the worker's armoury must be a strongly developed bump of irreverence. He must insist on the secular nature of all knowledge.

But not all sections of the British Labour movement possessed the intellectual insolence of the Welsh; the majority, in an act of collective surrender, rapturously submitted to Gaitskell's élitism and charm. In some ways Gaitskell's command, like that possessed by other charismatic leaders, resembled that of a hypnotist – using awe and love, a fatherlike authority and infallibility, and yet a caressing maternal tone which evokes the image of a mother wooing her child to sleep with a lullaby. Gaitskell's attractive voice was that of the woman successfully encapsulated within him. A charismatic leader is at once both father and mother and thus fulfils the eternal wish which man expresses in the myth that male and female were originally one. But such a leader's own inner balance can be precarious, for he must at all costs prevent his active domineering drives from being overcome by his more submissive, feminine and seductive tendencies. Gaitskell's constant struggle to enforce party discipline was a symptom of his own inner disorder and the impolitic rigidity with which he tried to impose changes upon the party's constitution and to alter Clause Four of that constitution revealed his lack of inner freedom.

This gave Gaitskell the appearance of operating mechanically and insensitively, and led Nye Bevan to hint, devastatingly, that he was a 'desiccated calculating machine'. But, for once, Nye's characteristically concrete imagery was confusing, for Gaitskell, paradoxically, was a deeply emotional man. He had found the power of the hydrogen bomb far too alluring, for he needed to identify with a powerful father image in order to protect himself from the threat of his own passivity. Perhaps some of that passivity arose from his identification with the Asian nurse who tended him for a short but decisive time in Burma, when he was an infant; certainly her influence was so strong that Gaitskell romantically and nobly imposed upon an uneasy Labour Party a totally unrealistic policy towards coloured and black immigrants that, electorally, was to make Labour pay a heavy toll for many years. That nurse was probably only one of a number of early influences that shaped the acquiescence within his character; and his need to ward off this disposition was to have important political consequences.

There will certainly be those who would prefer to dismiss the speculation that Gaitskell's extraordinary and unexpected passion for dancing and rock music perhaps provides clues to his constant need to be overassertive; it was certainly an odd interest for someone who presented so high-minded and severe a public persona. The dance, we must recall, is said to have its origins in the imitative movements by the tribe of the totem animal; that totem animal was the god/father of the primal horde who, in myth or fact, was killed and devoured by rebellious sons. Perhaps Gaitskell, in a show of innocent fun, could mask its totemistic intimations; it may be legitimate to ask if his interest was an acting out of some buried Oedipal rebellion. Could it be that the identification with the totem/god/father that moved the dancing guilty repentant sons of the tribal horde was echoed in Gaitskell's participation in the dance and the rock of his day? And is there a concordance between the extravagant identification within the tribal dance with the slain father and the evident identification with an overassertive father that was embossed on Gaitskell's personality? Be this as it may, what is indisputable, except by the purblind, is that Gaitskell's need to imitate a heavy-handed father, to play so affirmatively the rôle of leader, was psychologically overdetermined. His projection of this psychological need on to the Labour Party debates, particularly on the issue of Britain's retention of the H-bomb, acted as a detonator, and thus when I arrived in the House of Commons, the Parliamentary Labour Party was torn and bleeding.

His need was the source of his obsessional traits which exacerbated the internecine party conflict on the bomb issue and were to prove disastrous for the party. His determined aim to emancipate the Labour movement from its traditional orthodox ideology was pursued with the fanaticism of a heretic. There are always dangers in any movement which is bound together by a common philosophy. The phase of childhood development in which the child alternates between dependence on his mother and the assertion of his own autonomy so often finds echoes in adult life; if the parent group with whom the individual is identified insists upon his total subjugation then some, to survive, must assert independence. Gaitskell's obsessionalism required that party lines must be firmly laid down; but papal edicts lead to schisms. Under Gaitskell the rule books of the party had to be redrawn, no comma omitted and no 't' left uncrossed lest the new holy writ should be ill-defined. His intelligence and, even more, his charm enabled him to assert his authority but his fatal obsessional flaw meant that he had to fight every battle, never to concede an inch, to 'fight, fight and fight again'; in practice, of course, this meant he won every battle but the last. He himself was never to be prime minister and if he had not died when he did it is, in my view, unlikely that Labour would have gained sufficient unity to be able to govern in the 1960s.

However, during his ascendancy over the Labour Party, there is no doubt that Gaitskell fascinated some of the most intelligent of Labour MPs; some were extravagantly in love with him. The one-time Home Secretary Frank Soskice, with whom, as he at my request piloted in the Lords some of my social reforming Bills, I formed a close friendship, once told me, months after the event, that Gaitskell's death had extinguished all his joy in politics. And Bill Rodgers (now Lord Rodgers), with whom, despite his political vicissitudes I have always maintained a friendship, used all his considerable organisational skills to protect Gaitskell from assault; and, like Roy Jenkins, who in May 1996 during a television interview frankly declared he had loved Gaitskell, continues to resent any posthumous depreciation of his hero.

The taunt that Gaitskell had around him a 'magic circle', the so-called Hampstead group, was well founded, for every leader possessing charisma does use magic, the hermaphrodite quality which enthrals his followers, for they, like all of us, unconsciously yearn to be both man and woman at the same time. The moods of the leader, sometimes alternating, sometimes operating simultaneously, can have a fatal fascination when he displays both his male and female qualities, provoking awe and solace as he switches from awesome authority father to tender mother; his fascinated followers can swoon into submission. As in all human relationships, the phenomenon of interchange of rôles comes into existence, even as between man and woman and, indeed, even more markedly, in homosexual relationships. One partner can play the part of father, mother or child to the other, who, by identification or displacement, can also represent father, mother or child; and so, in like fashion, a double-triangular play can arise between the charismatic leader and his followers who, even while they submit to him, can also care for and protect him.

When Gaitskell waved his wand, he enchanted not only Wykehamists and Oxbridge men; tough trade union leaders fiercely protected him, and some of the most belligerent trade union MPs were his stoutest supporters. The support they had given him when they ensured in the leadership election of December 1955 that he received twice as many votes as Nye Bevan continued until his death. This unstinting approval of his policies was strangely toned; at his behest, the bellicose could become wondrously docile, and the obeisance yielded to him often came from the brightest among trade union MPs. I never ceased to wonder at Gaitskell's command over men like the redoubtable Charles Panell, an elderly tough trade union MP, with a personal biography so different from his, a man saved only by lack of formal education from the fate of becoming a brilliant lawyer or disputatious historian. Docile towards Gaitskell, his rage at private Parliamentary Labour Party meetings against those of us who refused to join the genuflexions to his idol was incandescent.

Such irrational motivation between leaders and led does not necessarily mean that charismatic leadership must inevitably lead to disaster. Provided a sense of reality and devotion to social aims are superordinate in the relationship, and provided the leader does not become intoxicated with power, the consequences can be benign. But charisma is a dangerous gift to possess. If the contending elements within the psychic life of the possessor are too precariously poised, and the inner balance between the active domineering and seductive strivings is felt to be at risk, then the charismatic leader can attempt to impose on others, as well as on himself, an excessive discipline; that is his only way to stay erect. Gaitskell's charisma had brought him the leadership of the Labour Party, but the authoritarian, intolerant and rigid style of leadership which he needed to maintain his own intactness was to deny him victory in the 1959 General Election. The country saw a party which had been divided by his provocations and was not prepared to give Labour its confidence.

When, a few years later, Gaitskell died at the young age of 57 there was much dispute over the nature of his enigmatic illness; but I would speculate that the answer to the mystery lies away from the varying medical diagnoses that have been proffered. In part, we encompass our own deaths. Gaitskell was no 'desiccated calculating machine', but he could give rise to a perception of himself as unbending and unremitting; in fact, the carapace he developed, although tough enough to protect him from external assault, was too frail to protect him from himself. Psyche and soma are rarely apart, and an internal psychic fracture or haemorrhage can and does find physical expression. Charisma, for some carriers, can be a fatal disease.

Charisma II:

Aneurin Bevan

There was no more compelling orator in Britain than the stutterer Aneurin Bevan. His was a remarkable lineage. From Moses to Demosthenes to Churchill, the eloquent stutterers have always been the most violent of men. God punished the stammering Moses for his ungovernable rage by refusing to permit this greatest leader of men ever to reach the Promised Land. Nye Bevan was to share a similar fate.

His oral aggression was feared by foe and friend alike. But he was no wild iconoclast; even his most destructive attacks on authority were ever accompanied by imaginative balms and soothing reparations. For this turbulent man, who once, with insight, described himself in a revealing private letter as 'so ill-balanced a vessel', yearned for calm, for peaceful havens and for what he so frequently called 'the serene society'. He loathed his own dis-ease, and his passionate and successful creation of the National Health Service was a marvellous bid by a man to heal himself by healing the nation.

When in my teens, sometimes I acted as chairman of Bevan's public meetings in Cardiff. The intergenerational rivalries that today are so ugly a feature of the competitive political scene in and out of Westminster had no place in the old South Wales Labour movement. Youngsters were encouraged to carry the torch; responsibility was thrust upon them, not grudgingly conceded, and it was considered fit that a committed young man should have the honour to preside over the large gatherings that, in those pre-television days, Nye Bevan's presence assured. For me, those occasions when I sat beside Nye were not necessarily easy moments. The awaiting audience was never listless; it was seized with expectancy, and the pitch of the chairman's introductory remarks had to chime with the mood that enveloped the hall. A prologue, devoid of histrionics, but never so prosaic that it diminished the occasion, was demanded. And, during the towering orator's inspirational address, always a morality tale, always part-sermon, the text was to be carefully scanned, even as, simultaneously, I had to resist the magic of the wizard lest all detachment be lost and no reserve was available to control and bless the mass audience when, in the immediate aftermath of the speech, reluctantly it came out of the spell to face again the drudgery of the mundane.

Too young to have witnessed Bevan, Professor Dai Smith, in his remarkable study of the relationship between the South Wales culture and Bevan's unique contribution to British politics, has studied a film of Bevan in the 1950s which showed him

> leaning forward, half-engaged in an over the garden wall conspiracy with his audience, disinclined to harangue where the whisper will have the listener striving to be in on the act. The gestures he makes are small-scale and friendly. The pauses are those of the metronomic master of timing, his tone is sweet and reasonable, confiding and bemused. There is the swoop, of body and of meaning, into a demotic mode that removes the platform between speaker and assembled until he has deflated pretensions and restored the arcane to the democracy, and all without descent into populist know-nothingness.

The extraordinary choreography which accompanied Bevan's delivery contained, however, one gesture which I feared. When he warmed up and the Welsh *hwyl* began, when the voice lost all its sweetness and mounted to a feminine falsetto, he would repeatedly take out his handkerchief from his breast pocket and wipe it deliberately across his mouth. Then I would squirm uneasily in my seat and wonder whether Nye would be successful in smothering the forbidden words, while the reporters below would expectantly hold their pencils and, looking up at the platform, hopefully await another indiscretion.

Unhappily, too frequently, he did not fail them, for his oral aggression sometimes could not only inflict havoc upon his opponents but, as with his notorious anti-Tory 'vermin' speech, could recoil upon his party and his colleagues. His handkerchief gesture was a symbolic attempt to stifle his own aggression, for he feared it himself; but the block in his speech betrayed in starker fashion that fear of his own violence. In part his stammer was an unconscious attempt to regulate his intemperate attacks.

But it was that falsetto voice emerging from that huge man which told of his diversity. None can doubt his identification with his forceful mother. He emblazoned, in his feminine identification, the ethos of what young political pups now patronisingly describe as 'Old Labour', for that party was essentially mother-orientated. It was the welfare party, maternally concerned, the comforter, the nurse, the bountiful. The great divide between that party, which gave Britain the welfare state and the National Health Service, and the Tories was that the Conservatives were essentially father-orientated, basically authoritarian in mood, believing in an élite, at ease in a structured fag system and only restless with their Whips when, as in John Major's case, the leader fails to provide the dominance which they crave and which Thatcher, the phallic woman garbed in hermaphrodite finery, as father surrogate did provide.

But a price is often paid by a male mother-orientated orator: his passionate orality can seduce his audiences, but, lacking sufficient emphases, when called upon to face an individual woman he fumbles. His private hesitations and problems then may become enmeshed in the public domain. There, an aggressive, masterful and compelling display of eloquence, overdetermining the essential femininity of the speaker and compensating for the private personal inadequacy, can, as with Nye Bevan, be speedily followed by imaginative and healing reparation. Often, however, the rhetoric of the sexually inadequate can have catastrophic results, as that great orator Adolf Hitler, whose speeches took millions to hell, only too chasteningly demonstrated. Despite Hitler's masculine show of uniforms, big boots and spurs, he certainly did no more than fumble in private with the pathetic Geli, his half-sister's daughter, who shot herself; and Eva Braun, though she tried to shoot herself for love of Hitler, never found before or after the episode a fully potent lover. But consolation for private impotence may be found in the sense of multi-potency to be derived from the highly charged intro-active group situation of the huge public meeting, where the orality of the orator can bring temporary balm to his deeply wounded self-esteem, and bring him the full response which he has found himself incapable of prompting from an individual woman. Public but not private orgasms can thus be achieved.

Hitler's macho display as he bound his huge homoerotic assemblies to him was a masquerade; essentially he was the great seducer. And although in Nye Bevan's case the consequences were as benign as Hitler's were malignant, his goal when facing a large audience of men was also to achieve a consummation. Four-letter words were shunned in his days and sexual intercourse was described, coyly, as 'an act of intimacy'; that was the euphemism Bevan himself borrowed when he made explicit the technique he was using to captivate his listeners. The audience of the political speaker, he wrote,

> will never give their hearts and minds to him if he appears alien either by manner, matter or by the remoteness of his illustrations. If he is strange there will be no intimacy and intimacy based on mutual sympathy is the essence of successful advocacy. He must therefore belong to those whom he is trying to persuade, belong in the profoundest sense of the term.

And by 'belonging' Bevan, at least unconsciously, was revealing that in his speech-making he was engaged in a wooing that went far beyond that of a class warrior identifying with his class. He rightly insisted that he was using the term in the most profound sense. He was not seeking the token votes of his audiences; he was seeking their hearts. 'The first function of a political leader,' he once wrote, 'is advocacy. It is he who must make articulate the wants, the frustrations and the aspirations of the masses. Their hearts must be moved by his words, and so his words must be attuned to their realities.'

It was to the hearts of men rather than women that he made his appeal; this was the need of his habitude as of his temperament, for he was following his earliest practice when all his speeches had been addressed to totally homogeneous audiences composed entirely of miners. And, as he began, so he persisted, never haranguing or commanding; his conquests were made more subtly with a feminine guile. He could, and did, play the coquette and, never brusquely but with immensely teasing foreplay, simultaneously brought himself and his audience, after so much intellectual romping and laughter, to a joyous climax.

The encapsulation of the mother, which played so considerable a determinant in Bevan's disposition, was, within the culture of South Wales, no idiosyncrasy. 'Mam' in the valleys had her own privileged domain in the home, where, in the Bevan household, Phoebe Bevan regally presided; although women overwhelmingly voted as their fathers and husbands, and did not overtly enter in any way into the union and political life of their townships, their influence was singularly pervasive. These cultural factors must be taken into account before reductively attributing Bevan's mark-edly feminine orientation simply to imperfectly resolved Oedipal situations. Nevertheless it is impossible not to infer that the little Nye's secret relationship with his mother must have been intense, and that the corollary of such an attachment – the fear that punishment would come from the father if the secret was uncovered – gives us the clue to understanding the dynamic behind so many of Bevan's political stances.

Nye Bevan's father, in reality, was a gentle dreamy man, a most unlikely contender for the rôle of the destroyer who would eliminate a son suspected of clandestine incestuous desires; but the clinicians have long since taught us of how amidst the ambivalences afflicting the infant during the agonising Oedipus rite of passage, so often imperfectly negotiated, monsters can be fantasised that will haunt the adult throughout his life. Even as the ambivalences and oscillations of mood of the infant can lead to him both wanting and fearing to become the father's lover, so too, among the impossibilities that have in the end to be renounced in the real world although never totally extinguished in the unconscious, is the desire to possess the mother which brings the ultimate fear of violence, of castration, to be inflicted by the father.

All through his political life Nye Bevan, fearing that buried desire may provoke elimination, sought to pre-empt the threat; he defended himself against the anticipated retaliation of authority by launching repeated attacks upon authoritarian figures and institutions. His stammer had protected him from the consequences of the outbursts he would otherwise have made against his fecund father, who had, as children jealously in love with their mother often prefer to imagine, forced his wife to have ten children; but as soon as he could find a substitute father against whom he could release his violence, then the stammer was insufficient to inhibit it and with physical violence he fell upon his hapless headmaster. When I was young, I heard firsthand in Nye's home town legendary stories of his fights with the unfortunate man; and anyone who heard, as I have, Nye talk privately of schoolmasters and formal education would not forget the extravagances of his attacks, and could hardly fail to appreciate how powerful was the violence he carried as a child. Fortunately for our society that violence was later to be transmuted, with devastating effects, into oral attacks upon the evils of capitalism.

He was, of course, an orator for his pre-television time, when immediacy was demanded, when the artificiality of overprepared speeches was rightly suspect, when more than sound-bites was required; it was the time when spontaneity was all, when meditation and brooding may have preceded the speech but then would come the grand impromptu with the vitality of the unconscious propelling the orator. Now the autocue takes over the speaker, and the politicians are reduced to the rôle of second-rate actors. They become what Nye Bevan, once stressing the distinction between political speakers and actors, described as 'fundamentally mimes subordinated to their parts in a performance'; and as performing actors, of course, they require décor, stage lighting, cosmetic treatments, designer advice, Sheffield razzmatazz. Those of us belonging to Old Labour took our agitations to the streets, spoke on our soapboxes and makeshift podiums in the parks, plinths and ramshackle halls of our towns, with no props, no amplifiers; we depended on our passions, our language and our authenticity to establish a rapport with those we sought to convince. If our freedom from constraint meant that we often made intellectual errors, they at least belonged to us; the shameless vicariousness of our present-day politicians was no part of our communication.

With Bevan his communication did not, however, necessarily reach women. Certainly in Wales, on his own pitch, within a culture well accustomed to the denunciations and diatribes of the *offeiriads* and lay preachers of the chapels, eloquence was not rare and therefore was not overvalued; they were familiar with the pulpit histrionics of preachers who, with voices nicely tuned to crack with grief and passion, harangued racked congregations. So women left their menfolk to their high-flown talk, and let them soar to the stars in their lodges while they at home kept their feet well on the ground. In crises and strikes their loyalty was absolute and supportive; but Mams treated their men as chattering little boys and did not always regard their talk with high seriousness. And indeed the Welsh mothers had good cause to be sceptical of rodomontade. When I became the Member of Parliament for Nye's neighbouring constituency, I saw how ironic it was that the grim conditions of the tumbledown hospitals and housing in the valleys of Monmouthshire, a county which had enjoyed, through Nye Bevan, a Member who had commanded the Ministries of Health and of Housing, had contributed to an infant mortality rate which was one of the worst in the kingdom; and indignant that there was in my constituency a slothful acceptance of these unnecessary deaths, my earliest and not unsuccessful campaigns were demands for remedial responses. But Nye Bevan could hardly be regarded as a great constituency Member. There were strange ambivalences on Nye's part to his birthplace; and just as all of us show an impatience towards the foibles of an elderly mother that we would willingly indulge in other old ladies, so Nye in many ways showed more concern for the nation than his own area. Tredegar and Ebbw Vale were too constricting, as had been his assertive mother; and Nye went soaring among the stars rather than forage around the coal tips. In any event, Bevan's uncompromising radicalism and demand for change were, and not only for women in Wales, too revolutionary for a generation of women more sceptical and conservative and much more resistant to any upheaval, whatever promised betterment might be attained by the result.

But most men listening to Bevan were certainly beguiled by his hermaphrodite qualities. The raillery against, and the deflation of, unthinking authority, charged with violence but tempered by the solace and hope that in the most delicate and feminine of tones he brought them, were often irresistible and they succumbed, for with men he was at ease, even as with women he was often more awkward; his bumpy childless marriage to the spirited and handsome Jennie Lee had, I think, a brother and sister quality, and his domestic arrangements which led to his mother-in-law, with whom the couple lived, looking after them like children, no doubt corroborated the marital mood. Unlike Gaitskell, Bevan was no womaniser; what I believe he always wanted from women was the admiration that, in sibling rivalry in an overcrowded household, he had sought from his harassed mother and which, until her early death, he had gained from his sister Margaret May.

There was an occasion, precipitated by Nye, which explicitly spelled out to me this particular need. It occurred long before I came into the Commons. Shortly after I had become a solicitor and had, as a young man, opened my law practice in Cardiff, I received a message from Nye Bevan. He wished me to give an interview to an American woman academic who was with him in his nearby constituency of Ebbw Vale. She had, by his arrangement, been for a week with Harold Wilson observing his constituency, and then had been invited by Nye to join him for a similar time. The background to the granting of these facilities to the American was that she was engaged in writing a work on 'Bevanism' and, naïvely, had visited the Gaitskellite-manned Labour Party headquarters at Transport House, where she was rebuffed in her enquiries, and was told that she was attempting to scrutinise a phenomenon which did not exist. Undeterred, she had bearded Nye Bevan in the Commons and he had encouraged her to pursue her study. It would assist if, now that she had spent time with the left-wing leaders, she met someone articulate at the grass roots, and would I please oblige during the day she intended to spend in Cardiff. That day I was in the courts defending a murderer and did not relish the prospect of being distracted by some high-minded, grim but no doubt worthy American woman academic. I explained my difficulties but yielded, agreeing, unenthusiastically, to see her for a very short time during the court's lunch-time adjournment.

Her arrival made me curse my spurning the serendipity bestowed upon me by Bevan. To my surprise, she was an extraordinarily pretty young woman endowed with the arresting dark appearance of her Macedonian ancestors, and far removed from the stereotype of the aggressive and opinionated American woman academic that, in my misogyny, I had anticipated. Graceful, disconcertingly direct and full of generous laughter which made her sharp mind more acceptable and much less abrasive, with our shared interests I responded to her as any young man would. B was not content with a short interview and decided to pursue her 'studies' for a while in Cardiff, and, fortunately for me, I was the object of the study. We became lovers and spent a holiday together before she went back to the States with the intention of returning, her thesis completed, in six months' time; our relationship was not meant to be ephemeral. The artist whom I was to meet before B's return had, however, other ideas; she became my wife, and so I was saved from the terrifying fate of having a politically ambitious spouse.

It was some 30 years before I was to see B again. An American matron accompanying Harold Wilson in the Commons broke away from him to speak to me. To my discredit, I fear recognition on my part came slowly. But ever since their first meeting Wilson, I discovered, had remained in touch with B, meeting her when he was in the States and when, very occasionally, she came to Britain. Perhaps it was not surprising; she had been a dazzling young woman, and Wilson, as ever more talk than passion, evidently retained some romantic attachment, as ill-defined as when she had first met him.

But with Nye Bevan it had been otherwise; and she had never renewed the original acquaintance. He had liked the attention of the admiring young woman but his response to her had been one of Victorian propriety; I believe that was occasioned not by discipline but disinclination.

He was, in fact, more comfortable with a woman within a formal framework. He could not easily give what he felt he had never received, for Bevan, surprising as it may seem, despite all the acclamation and myriad acquaintances, was essentially a lonely man. He always carried an acute sense of deprivation, insisting 'so few people have given me anything'. Reared in a household teaming with competitive siblings, he evidently felt that he had not received his fair share of mother-love. Doubtless displacement of those feelings led him to empathise with all those born into a disadvantaged class, but it also meant that his relationship with women was hesitant, for, initially, he had, like all at the breast, wanted boundless love and this he felt had been cruelly denied him. The reciprocity for which he yearned was to be of a different order; it was established with his male audiences and with the extraordinarily delicate relationships he could, very exceptionally, establish with an admired male friend.

A footnote in a letter in 1930 from Nye Bevan to John Strachey, the great political educator to my generation, a man whose friendship I was later privileged to enjoy, is indeed revelatory:

> You are very good to me, John. It hurts me a little that you give so much and I can give you nothing in return. So few people have given me anything that I feel a little strange and bewildered.
>
> I count on our friendship as the one thing of value that membership of Parliament has given me. And yet as this friendship grows and becomes more and more part of me, I find myself becoming fearful. I am so conscious of bringing to our relationship nothing of value, and therefore am frightened of trusting so much of my affection in so ill-balanced a vessel.
>
> Please forgive me for exposing so shy a feeling to the peril of words. It is your generous nature that moves me to speak even though I know that speech will bruise you where it could caress.

Nye certainly knew speech could caress as well as abuse; that is what was felt by his audiences as he enfolded them while attacking his and their enemies. The same mood that bathed his relationship with Strachey enveloped his public meetings. The screaming 'outing' by today's small group of disturbed gays, unable to come to terms with their destiny and wanting to minimise their felt guilts by unloading their burdens on others who prefer the privacy of their sexual orientation, has lamentably contributed to a wider acting out of the homosexual component that Freud has insisted is part of all our natures, but which can often be so benignly sublimated. Even as the homosexual component in a man's nature can play so enriching a rôle with a woman, helping him to understand and so form a deeper relationship with her, so too, as so evidently with Bevan, it can intellectually light up a male friendship and, through

understanding and sympathy, bring succour and hope to
political congregations.

The prurient and the philistine may wilfully regard an
exploration of the qualities of charisma which leads to an
acknowledgement of the hermaphrodite disposition of the
political leader as an advertisement of such a leader's overt
bisexuality. Such a misinterpretation fails to acknowledge that
the hermaphrodite quality gives to leader and led the advantage
of understanding and of being understood, that the issue is one
of hermeneutics not homosexuality, not of sex but of sensibility.

But the prim and the timid are in one respect right in
suspecting a scandal, for the hermaphrodite leader uses his
charisma to provoke a metaphysical scandal. Not for him an
adjustment to 'reality' or the espousal of policies that reduce him
to a seismograph, passively responding to the blinkered
prejudices contained in the latest opinion poll. He is not
anchored to the present, for he is determined to shape the
future; and that requires him, when he speaks to the masses, to
use the heretical grammar of Isaiah and the prophets of Israel,
the enforcement of the future tense, the extension of language
over time.

Such talk, of course, is dangerous. It can lead to awesome
follies, like a belief, acted upon, in the 'thousand years Reich';
but it can also lead to the fulfilment, at least in part, of the
dreams of Martin Luther King, who shared his vision with
America: 'I have a dream that one day this nation will rise up,
live out the true meaning of its creed: we hold these truths to be
self-evident, that all men are created equal.' Such visionary
metaphysical scandals cannot only defy time but, we know, as
we witness the ingathering of Jews from Iraq, Ethiopia and
Georgia to a new State of Israel, and the creation of Mandela's
South Africa, that they can too defy geography. Bevan's
millenarianism was of that ilk; he was possessed of a vision of
socialist Britain. He did not regard 'the vision thing' as a
commodity to be hired from public relations firms.

Far from being shackled to an anachronistic past, Bevan's

opposition to the acquisitive revisionism of Gaitskell was not the bathos of nostalgia or the pathos of sentiment; it lay in his dream of a richer, more generous future. Doubtless, within his interpretation of the history of the working class, to which in his speeches he repeatedly returned, he found some assurance of a possible political destiny for Britain's workers; but there was no Marxist assumption of inevitability. The past pointed the direction to the future – he was most certainly not a 'here and now' man – but the lesson he took from history was that the future could be shaped by the living, human will. This hero of Old Labour was not resistant to change; he was no dinosaur and contemporary modernisers, so eager to jettison their party's traditions as detritus, need to note the distinction he drew between opportunism and a readiness to change, between political rewards and political achievements:

> The student of politics must ... seek neither universality nor immortality for his ideas and for the institution through which he hopes to express them. What he must seek are integrity and vitality. His Holy Grail is the living truth, knowing that being alive the truth must change. If he does not cherish integrity then he will see in the change an excuse for opportunism, and will exchange the inspiration of the pioneer for the reward of the lackey.

Now, however, the citadels of socialism which Bevan attempted to defend are being spattered with the graffiti of these self-acclaimed modernists; their sprawl, their slogans, their poverty-stricken language, are so often the efforts of immature children fulminating against the founding fathers. They mock the socialist veterans as quaint, as anachronisms; but how fuliginous is their abuse. Devoid of fierce confrontation, of the élan, of the magic that are the possessions of the charismatic, their precious sound-bites are mere nibbles; how miserably muted are their cautious responses to the contemporary human predicament. The words offered – justice, communality – become increasingly abstract, desperately governed by a bid for consensus; at all costs conflict must be avoided. The old socialist Utopia was to be achieved by struggle, by class warfare, but that is now deemed distasteful. Violent language must be eschewed, the concrete imagery of a Bevan declared embarrassing; petty bourgeois southern English gentility is the mode. Gone is the understanding that no orator can change the world without verbal violence, for, like Bevan, he has always depended upon his aggression; indeed, the aetiology of his rhetorical capacity reveals his oratory as a defence against his dangerous rages. Did not Freud teach us that civilisation began when man first hurled abuse not spears?

And so now we find ourselves not inspired but dispirited as we are offered words, words that are worn, threadbare, filed down; words that are the carcasses of words, phantom words, and too many of the modernisers, aping their Tory contemporaries, in between their elocution lessons, drearily chew and regurgitate the sound of them between their jaws. Their rehearsals are far removed from the ruminations of Bevan before he made a speech. He did not sit at the feet of any university professor of rhetoric but no politician in my lifetime more successfully achieved, as he often did, the Ciceronian union of wisdom and eloquence that teaches, delights and moves men to virtuous living; intuitively Bevan acknowledged the exalted world that Cicero assigned to rhetoric, a word now used so carelessly and, usually, pejoratively. For Cicero, as for Bevan, the orator's life was a discipline undertaken with all the seriousness of a semi-religious vocation. The skills of the rhetor, which in late antiquity were the very basis of diplomatic, military and administrative careers, are the skills which Bevan sought to acquire. He would not have demurred from Cicero's instruction:

> One needs a grounded knowledge of the most varied things, so as not to rattle off meaningless words for others to mock at. One needs to shape one's discourse, not only culling but collocating effectively. One needs to read others' motives, to the very depths of human nature,

since tickling or soothing anxieties is the test of a speaker's impact and technique. One should have at hand, as well, poise and the play of wit, an educated bearing, swift short ways of deflecting others' challenges or launching one's own, along with an understated gracefulness and sophistication ... And do I have to mention the delivery itself – how the body is controlled, its gestures, facial expressions, vocal inflections and modulations? Or need I emphasise memory, where all of this is filed away? Unless this stands guard over the material collected and elaborated, the material will evaporate, no matter how precious it was in itself.

Aneurin Bevan had, of course, never been tutored in the classics; he was in the same position as, lamentably, with the demise of classics in schools, most of the younger politicians now find themselves. Latin and Greek were part of the cement which helped to hold together the consciousness of nation and provided some continuity across generations; that bonding was part of the speeches of Gladstone and Disraeli. Bevan, nevertheless, although beyond the acquisitive reach of Hellenic articulation, which now seems, after so many centuries, to have found its limits, was, like Lloyd George, within reach of a rich Hebrew articulation, for this determinedly secular man had been cradled in the chapel culture, now dying, of the Welsh mining valleys; and his style and vocabulary so often revealed its source. Tony Blair, for a short while after his mother's death, may have spent his nights in consolatory readings of the Bible and he may make known his church-going, provoke dissent by sending his son to an élitist Roman Catholic school, interpolate, as a sound-bite, a well-worn pacific from the New Testament – never the Old, for that would be too conflictual – but essentially his is the language of the adman's copy; his vocabulary does not suggest that he finds the language of the Bible the main source of inspiration in the expression of his political views.

Increasingly, for many the Bible is becoming a closed book. That is not simply an aesthetic loss for our society; it is a severe deprivation, for the language of our politicians is now that of the sociological and economic textbooks. We find speeches are inflicted upon us that are often well researched, delivered fluently, but are, of course, dreary, unimaginative, passionless addresses; they lack the 'vitality' which Bevan well understood must inform the speeches of leaders if they are to inspire their followers to deeds and selflessness which can create a society more worthy of their humanity.

Many were the times I heard Bevan make vital, unpopular, tactless speeches, but never a populist one; he was an educator not a demagogue. The Labour Party modernisers who would dismiss his philosophy as outmoded, lacking relevance, boast about their capacity to face reality, but their vocabulary betrays them; their mode of expression, unlike his, is abstract rather than concrete, general rather than specific, periphrastic rather than direct. That acute French nineteenth-century political commentator de Tocqueville long since divined how language, when yielding excessively to what he described as the 'democratic dispensation', freed from the need to shape speech not by the standards of a particular class or circle but rather adapted for general acceptance by the overwhelming majority, degenerated in America into populism; and the consensus, conflict-free propositions of the political modernists here in Britain tell us that they are the most extreme of populists. Rabid crowd-rousing is not the only weapon the populist can select to command support.

Contrasting Bevan's pithiness with the linguistic flatulence of the modernisers is, therefore, no mere literary exercise. Words are the tools of thought. If they lose efficiency, that is, meaning, thought itself deteriorates. Thought can only be as precise as language lets it be. If the politicians' words are bloated, continuously euphemistic, then, in power, muddled action will assuredly follow. Euphemism is the effort of the well-meaning to avoid hurting others' feelings; in private discourse it may have justification, but when used by politicians it must be seen as suspect. A Labour Party denying its socialism, and unashamedly stealing Tory clothes in order to appear inoffensive to all, may claim respectability but, in fact, becomes a strumpet of a party, for what are being proffered are fantasies, fairy stories, the delusion that without struggle, without conflict, we can have a society where we can live happily ever after.

Bevan's philosophy infuriated many precisely because he identified and underlined the fundamental conflicts that he believed were endemic to a capitalist society; there was to be no smudging of the issues and the elusive serene society he sought could be reached only by forever increasing the tempo of the struggle. But it would be a misinterpretation to suggest that he was just another wager of class war, albeit an eloquent one. No major politician whom I have known, apart from John Strachey, was more aware of the interior life of man; and he understood that all external changes would be of no avail unless modifications came into our personal vision and conduct; he regarded man as man, and turned away with disgust from those whose political dogmas too often treated man as consumer or productive unit.

Not long before his death, in the 1959 post-election Labour conference, in one of his greatest speeches, Bevan reaffirmed his belief that it is the human condition that must be addressed if needed society changes are to be made. Seeking to rouse a dispirited Labour Party, he told the delegates that the principal task now was 'to enlarge and expand the personalities of our young men and women' so that, despite growing material prosperity, they 'again became conscious of the limitations and constrictions that the vulgar, affluent, meretricious society imposed upon them'. And he gave a warning, never more apposite than today, not to adjust policy opportunistically to pollster findings telling us how resistant electors are to criticism of consumerism; with superb arrogance, he denied the proposition that the reasons given by those who voted against Labour in 1959 should necessarily be respected: 'Are we really now to believe that the reasons that people give for their actions are the causes of their actions? Such a naïve belief in the rational conduct of human beings would wipe out the whole of modern psychology.' Bevan was insightfully seeking a society more sensitive to the deeper needs of men and women; he believed that an expanding shopping-list was no answer to their personal predicaments or to the ills of society. And he instructed the delegates not to yield to the contemporary mood but to teach, to preach: 'The problem is one of education, not of surrender!' His charisma enveloped the hall and once again I witnessed him galvanising his audience to fight, and not accommodate.

That he could capture the imagination of the delegates and give them renewed hope, was in part due to his selection of words; for this stammerer had at his disposal a hard-won vocabulary. Up to his mid-20s, determined to avoid the pitfalls of his stutter, he had pored almost every night over his *Roget's Thesaurus* searching for synonyms that would not trip his tongue. Moreover, in part, the responses he obtained came from his prophetic stance; he was the preacher of the valleys exhorting and commanding his congregation to fight the good fight, for only by fighting would Jerusalem be theirs. But physical disadvantage and South Wales culture do not in themselves explain Bevan's magic; that sprang from the quality of hermaphroditism which suffused that last conference speech. His imperiousness induced awe, his mellifluous cradling, solace; from one human being the audience received both paternal instruction and maternal succour.

Thus his audiences could leave his presence with their self-esteem lifted and their hope increased and, for a short while, fitfully, the warm tides flowing between him and his listeners could soothe him too, giving him what his divided nature denied him: 'serenity'. Exteriorising that profound need, the conflict-ridden man, using an adjective unfamiliar to political practitioners, repeatedly insisted that the ultimate goal of the true socialist was 'the serene society'; but, reflecting his own interior battles, he also asserted that that could be reached only by unremitting political struggle.

For Bevan, the private predicament and society's dilemmas

were all as one. In singular form, he was acting out, for all our benefits, the biological imperative that some psychoanalysts have suggested govern us: the law of psychic homoeostasis. That decree instructs us that we have, inbuilt, a psychological system which seeks to attain a steady mental state, a condition of dynamic balance.

Such harmony was to be denied to Bevan. His exigent desire to have a united party fighting and winning the general election of 1959 led him to capitulate to Gaitskell and renounce his allegiance to unilateral nuclear disarmament; his action dismayed his allies, failed in its objective, and killed him. Although he rallied his party in his unforgettable 'meretricious society' conference speech of 1959, he could not sustain himself. When I entered Parliament, I found him in a dangerously depressed mood. No longer able with the old freedom to play monarch in his court, no longer surrounded by his old friends and admirers in his special corner of the House of Commons smoking-room, he prowled around the corridors engulfed in gloom. His participation in debates became perfunctory and revealed too often a lack of preparation. Locked up within himself he could not shift his attention to new controversies. His attacks were no longer reserved for the political enemy; they were upon himself, and it was often hard physically to be near him without sensing his melancholic withdrawal. The end was inevitable. To unleash such massive aggression, as was his endowment upon himself, meant cancer and death. He was to die as a result of fall-out, as certainly as if the bomb had been dropped.

And, with his death, whatever curbs might have been placed on the mercenaries of modern capitalism, all hope of a genuinely socialist Britain died too. Only he had the capacity to provide a charismatic leadership capable of fending off the temptations of the affluent slavery proffered by an unthinking technology. He alone in the Labour movement had the magic to persuade a people to choose the holy land, not the fleshpots of Egypt. However Britain is to be reshaped, his untimely death

guaranteed it was never to be in the image of the founding
fathers of the Labour Party.

Now indeed, if a charismatic leader of Bevan's order was
available, he would probably be entrapped by television. It is
chasteningly paradoxical that when an orator-leader has for the
first time in history the opportunity to speak not to thousands
but to tens of millions, no politician can move the nation as their
predecessors succeeded in the last century and earlier part of this
century. With the death of Mitterrand, I doubt whether, in our
television age, it will ever be possible to say again of any
European politician as *Le Monde* in 1995 said of the French
President: 'What he wanted to do, and what he has more or less
achieved, was never to lose sight of literature in the smallest
details of political life. One felt this profound coquetry in his
speeches, where he offered himself the luxury, as did de Gaulle,
of rehabilitating an unusual and charming word.'

Television quenches such elegance; its debilitating demands
can drain even the most distinguished of rhetoricians. Michael
Foot, a great wordsmith, and in his day and moment a superbly
bellicose parliamentary orator, on becoming leader, was trapped
by his integrity. Overburdened with the circumspection
leadership imposed and compelled to conform to the orthodox
canons of television, with his aggression consequently mortified
and his spontaneity suppressed, he lost his freedom and thus,
rather than participate in television's mendacious advertising
techniques, he became dumb; the public misinterpreted his
condition as inadequacy, and Thatcher hugely benefited.
Producers made him, as other politicians, victim of their sly
counsel to tread softly, to remember he is speaking to the little
old lady in her front room; he must simulate intimacy, speaking
as to one or two, although he knows he is talking to millions. Is it
any wonder it so often sounds as spurious as it is? On a public
stage the inauthentic politician, lacking the marvellous
self-created choreography of a Lloyd George or Bevan, could,
nevertheless, with some effect, borrow the props of the large
gesture and extravagance; but, lacking props and encouraging

reverberations from a visible audience, a mimetic exercise in intimacy is so often beyond his histrionic talent, and the resulting dissonances jar upon the listener.

The spin doctors, that odious breed now parasitically clinging to our political process, aware that increasingly the public senses the deception, have, in more recent years, devised for their puppets a new *mise-en-scène*. A more successful confidence trick can be played out if the political leader is televised boldly addressing, with the unseen autocue, a set meeting of adulatory followers; or a meeting so arranged that it is certain there will be a small dissenting minority who, to the applause of the selected majority, the leader will relentlessly crush. The repertoire of imposture is continuously extended as pliant journalists at televised 'press conferences' question the politicians who authoritatively read out the pre-prepared answers. And now, in 1996, the circle has turned full circle; Major follows Blair to meet people on the streets. Once we in Old Labour went to the street corner and from our soapbox, as agitators, we endeavoured to educate; today, accompanied by television crews, the politician paces a stretch of the high street and rushes through the supermarket. We communicated; they perform.

Meantime, the Commons has been demeaned as genuine debate ceases. Rules now insist that often speeches must be short, and the Speaker, under pressure from MPs insistent that their constituents must see their faces, maintains a rigid roster; prepared speeches for TV and the local paper, often drafted by research workers paid out of the MPs' excessive expense allowance, are hurriedly recited in the intervals between, in the case of many Tory MPs, looking after outside commercial interests. Ministers opt for the *Today* programme rather than the dispatch box, and Prime Minister's Question Time becomes a charade, a mere slot in the week's television programmes.

Within such a degraded political world, the possibilities of the emergence of a charismatic leader, possessed of a sense of reality and a devotion to social aims, diminish. The political failure of Michael Foot, a pure man with selfless commitment, reveals how someone with such a potential becomes a misfit in a society that is so awry, so incorrigibly narcissistic. The man or woman who subliminally may be felt to encapsulate some of the qualities of both the firm, infallible, all-powerful father and those of a glorified, provident mother is a threat to the Narcissus who at all costs wants to avoid the painful graduation into adulthood that a family unit demands. When hermaphrodite leadership so beckons, the Narcissus retreats.

In a society tutored by Thatcher to glorify individualism, narcissism is sanctioned, immaturity is tenaciously grasped. Now, however, whereas Foot, to his great credit, failed to relate to that wretched society, Blair is dramatically succeeding; Foot was the misfit but Blair clicks in. Clearly the 'magic' which Blair dispenses must be of a different order from that which has sprung from the charismatic Labour leaders of the past. Twenty-first-century Britain seems set to produce a new phenomenon in democratic political leadership; but, in our eagerness to be free of the decrepitude of Tory government, are we overattracted by the novelty? Is there some strange and disturbing congruence between the pathology of our society and the configuration of Blair's psyche?

Androgynous Politics:

Tony Blair

Warning: You Are Entering
a Conflict-Free Zone

Early in 1984 during the passage of a Bill pretentiously entitled 'The Matrimonial and Family Proceedings Bill', I had my first encounter with the newly arrived Member, Tony Blair. This government Bill was a very tardy and inadequate response to an agitation I had been conducting since 1979. It was in that year, ten years after I had succeeded, together with my Welsh colleague Alec Jones, in putting on the statute book the Divorce Reform Act which radically altered our medieval divorce laws, I commenced a campaign to remedy the many blemishes within my own Act.

It had been a long struggle throughout the 1960s to persuade the House that root and branch changes were required. When, in 1963, I made a bid to make some tentative changes which could mitigate at least some of the most oppressive features of the divorce laws, Church lobbies were too powerful for me, and my Bill reached the statute book in tatters. My renewed efforts in 1969 met with fierce criticism, but the wind of change was by then, at last, with me; but the swinging sixties were certainly not as swinging as popular mythology would have us believe. It was

53

a hard task to move Parliament away from the punitive, guilt-ridden doctrine of proof of matrimonial breakdown as a prerequisite to the grant of a divorce decree to the doctrine of matrimonial breakdown; and, in order to take the House with me, I had no alternative but to concede provisions relating to finance and to the measurement of guilt in determining financial settlements after divorce, which were either inappropriate or possessed a built-in obsolescence.

The opponents of reform, who wanted no change, had succeeded in arousing alarm and concern among wives who were persuaded that I was sponsoring a Bill which could leave them abandoned. Since, by my Bill, for the first time, it would become possible to divorce a wife without her consent if the marriage had broken down many years before, it was only possible to overcome the storm by agreeing to insert in the Bill a guiding rule to the courts that in divorce proceedings the parties to a divorce should be returned to the same financial position as they would have been in had there been no divorce. The rule was utterly impractical and often wholly inappropriate, but it was one of the prices I was forced to pay to obtain the 1969 Divorce Act.

Only now, in 1996, have we at last had an Act which removes some of the serious substantive blemishes which, knowingly, I was compelled to leave in my Act in order to secure its passage. I was, however, 15 years after my 1969 Act, able to achieve a considerable modification of the inequitable financial rule governing post-divorce financial settlements; for by then the rule was causing widespread injustices, particularly to the wives and children of second marriages, who found childless first wives, or those with no dependent children, were receiving a disproportionate amount of their former husbands' incomes.

I had anticipated in 1969 that in the end the accumulated grievances would be so weighty that alteration of the rule would become a political imperative. By 1979 I had received hundreds of letters blaming me for the financial injustices which people believed they were enduring. But I was not the only recipient of such letters. MPs were being pressurised by many of their constituents to alter the rules, and, indeed, not a few divorced MPs were themselves suffering from their harshness. By forming an all-party MPs group which I took repeatedly to the Lord Chancellor, Quintin Hogg – always sulky and irascible when dealing with divorce reform, for the wounds of his own divorce have never been healed – and after an equivocating report from the Law Commissioners, to whom the matter had belatedly been referred, the demand for change, backed by a motion that I persuaded 230 Members to sign, became overwhelming. Hogg, not a man to stay in a dangerously crumbling intellectual dug-out over long, ultimately conceded, and a remedial Bill was placed before the House.

When the principle of that Bill was debated in the second reading in the Commons, Blair did not participate; but the Whips, doubtless thinking it would be a useful blooding experience for a young Member, particularly one with the advantage of being a barrister, placed him upon the committee which now had the task of considering the Bill in detail. Unusually, the Bill was to be considered in two committee stages, for, not wishing to create new difficulties while resolving those unnecessarily caused by my 1969 Act, I had cajoled the government into using the procedure which enables a special standing committee to come into existence charged with the task of holding inquisitorial hearings on the detailed provisions of a Bill before subsequently, in a conventional committee, they are debated clause by clause before returning to the full House for ratification. This special procedure regrettably now appears to have fallen into desuetude; a painstaking audit of the human consequences of social and political acts is too onerous a task for our present-day 'professional' MPs, more concerned to gain attention by sound-bites than, in the shadows, to focus upon the details of legislation.

Today, too often, the false assumption is made that the task of politicians is, by way of exhortation and coercion, to resolve conflicts which have already arisen; rarely, however, do such techniques produce permanent reductions in the tension level in our society. The legislator content to be merely a safety-valve for social protest demeans himself; his rôle should be anticipatory, ready always to apply social energy to the abolition of the recurrent strains in our society. But these are days of instant politics, and the politics of prevention is unfashionable. Such a mood suits indolent MPs and an executive not wishing its proposals to be subject to unremitting scrutiny. The notorious fiasco that followed the passing of the Child Support Agency Act is certainly not the only recent testament to the well-intentioned but defective legislation now being enacted.

My participation, however, in the prolonged committee stages of the modest 1984 Bill gave me not only the opportunity to scrutinise in detail its content, but also, by chance, the opportunity to remark upon the youngster who was so rapidly to become the leader of my party. I have no doubt, however, that Blair's self-absorption made him unaware of my scrutiny. I do not share the view that first impressions are usually misleading; on the contrary, after decades of political experience, I believe increasingly, if not arrogantly, in the assessments I make in the immediacy of a first encounter, particularly with a politician. Freud once remarked: 'He who has eyes to see and ears to hear may convince himself that no mortal can keep a secret. If his lips are silent, he chatters with his fingertips; betrayal oozes out of him at every pore.' The eyes, of course, are not the only windows of the soul. Our frowns, tics and facial contortions are all part of the repertoire of emotions which are revealed and not concealed in our body language. Even as our handwriting is a seismograph, tapping out the secrets of our psyche, so the creases that involuntarily form upon our faces are loquacious messengers and even the masters of histrionics, actors and politicians, cannot dissimulate and mask their guilts and conflicts. The initial encounter with another is all-important; love or hate at first sight is not necessarily to be mocked. As time passes, the vision, no longer pristine, becomes blurred and faults are no longer noted; habitude dulls our original keen awareness, and attributes and blemishes fade out of view.

With Blair when, on the committee, I first met and talked to him, I was momentarily puzzled by the ambiguity of his mien. There was a dissonance between the athletic build of this clear-blue-eyed, six-foot-tall, good-looking man with classic broad shoulders tapering down to a narrow waist and the essential sinuosity within his bearing which became more pronounced as it was accompanied by an over-ready winsome little-boy smile. That night, telling my wife, as was my wont, the day's gossip in the House, I told her, as she reminded me some years later, that an intelligent young rock star had joined our committee. I had evidently believed myself to have picked up Blair's vibes; the androgynous quality that quintessentially belongs to Mick Jagger, a performer whose presentations played a significant part in Blair's life at Oxford, hovered and continues to hover around him. To have made so recklessly such a snap judgement, even if subsequent probings may provide persuasive corroboration, will, I am well aware, be regarded as preposterous by some biographers and political commentators, who, perhaps fearing their emotions, despise empathy and insist, despite the limitations of such assessments, on their overcerebral evaluations of public figures. Brushing aside what they mistakenly regard as trivial irrelevancies, they bury the real man under an avalanche of easily verifiable facts. They lack the wisdom that lies within the ancient hermeneutical Jewish tradition that contains a disinclination to measure a man with a foot-rule because the corpse is measured in this way for a coffin.

Even as I am writing, I note that the journalist Hugo Young, while reviewing in the *Guardian* the second volume of Thatcher's autobiography, cannot forbear in an aside to deprecate my psycho-biography of the former prime minister. The academic *manqué* literally belittles psycho-biography by shortening the noun to 'psycho-bio' but clearly cannot contain his vexation with himself that within his prolix biography of Thatcher, in all the 550 pages replete with facts, in no way did he note the significance of the omission in Thatcher's *Who's Who* entry of any reference to her mother. This omission, first remarked upon in my psycho-biography, was the clue that helped me to interpret so much of Thatcher's politics as the public consequence of a desperate effort on her part to erase her mother from her biography. Now Young, seemingly half-ashamed of his myopia, is honest enough to feel it necessary to point out that Thatcher has now, undoubtedly in response to my book, inserted in her latest volume a short paragraph attempting to ward off my diagnosis; there she belatedly and unconvincingly attempts to idealise her mother. But Hugo Young again misses the point, for he fails to notice that, significantly, nowhere in the index or content of Thatcher's volume will he find a mention of the dour, living-in martinet grandmother who dominated the Thatcher household during the first ten years of Margaret's life. Phoebe Stephenson is the woman who is taboo; she is the one who must not be named, the woman who left Margaret's mother, Beatrice, so stricken, so bereft, that, as I sought to show in my psycho-biography, her lack of affection left Margaret full of resentments that ultimately were to be startlingly worked out in the public affairs of Britain.

In myths parthenogenesis may occur; but in real life if politicians overtly or elliptically attempt the ablation of their parents or grandparents, only journalists illiterate in the field of psychodynamics could dismiss, or fail to notice, the political consequences that stem from such odd repudiations. Doubtless, just as some journalists piled up the 'facts' upon which they judged the former prime minister, so those of Hugo Young's ilk do likewise when they write of the future prime minister; they prefer to work on their simplicities rather than engage in the arduous task of identifying the concatenations which link a Thatcher to austere Phoebe Stephenson or a Blair to his outrageously promiscuous grandmother.

It was, however, secondary elaborations of Blair's basic psychic configuration that, in the committee stages of the Matrimonial Bill, arrested my attention. He had voted against this Bill on second reading and I found the coolness of this young newcomer to any implementation of its provisions, to which, with others, I had given so much thought and for which I had long striven, presumptuous. And it vexed me; it prompted me far more than I otherwise would have done to relate Blair's committee contributions to the man himself.

I noted his talent to combine a pronouncement of unexceptional banalities with a distaste to anchor them in the sordid detail of legislation: 'marriage should be viewed as a common endeavour, in a broader sense, as opposed simply to pounds, shillings and pence'. He wanted, he explained, the emphasis in the Bill to be changed so that the guiding principle of the Bill should be: 'that marriage is a common endeavour between man and woman'. Such a change of emphasis would have meant enacting meaningless mush and a retreat from wrestling, as was the whole purpose of the Bill, with the financial inequities my Divorce Act had bequeathed. I was impatient with this attempt to gloss over the realities of the conflictual situations which so often, unhappily, arise when a marriage breaks down and financial disputes abound. But Blair, by his approach, was giving to me my first intimation of his need to place himself and his politics in a conflict-free zone; he was clearly unhappy that we should be acknowledging the realities of the fierce marital struggles, expressed in pounds, shillings and pence, that wretchedly accompany many family breakdowns. I noted too the emotional overtones in his condemnation of my view that support should be given to a clause permitting the divorce court, when the funds within a marriage were available and when there were no children or when they were grown up, to order a complete and final distribution of the matrimonial assets. Blair eschewed the clean break which I advocated, a break which could encourage parties to build up new lives untrammelled by past or renewed financial obligations. Such an approach was blunt, unblurred, and did not commend itself to Blair's mindset; he abhorred the principle of the clean break. 'That principle,' the moralist told the house, 'shuffles off the lifelong responsibilities of marriage and brings a change in the nature of the marriage contract by permitting an easier clean break even where the parties may not consent.'

It was unpalatable for Blair to acknowledge that there are dead marriages, that conflict can be mortal, an acknowledgement that he was still reluctant to make in 1996, when the government at last presented a well-thought-out Bill to remedy the more substantive defects of my Divorce Act. Then, he muddied the waters rather than assisting forward a valuable Bill. In debates explicitly agreed to be governed by a free vote, Blair sought to taunt the government and accuse them of disarray when one of the Lord Chancellor's clauses was defeated. A justifiably angry John Major accused Blair, as did *The Times* and many others less partisan, of being unprincipled. The charge was inappropriate; Blair was acting according to the prejudices of his principles, which he had already displayed in 1984, when he wished to have in statutory form an idealised mutuality and an avoidance of acknowledgement of strife, a wish which reflected his essential mode of thought: all differences of views should be minimised.

Recently the psychoanalyst Riccardo Steiner, noting the havoc this wish for spurious consensus can bring, insisted that:

> what is necessary for dialogue is not to accept compulsorily and arrive at a common idea of what is true and valid, but rather to accept the importance and the necessity of a genuine dialogic attitude in reaching a view ... proper dialogue is far more important than formal agreement or consensus – the latter can simply function not to fuse but to confuse horizons and to prevent thought.

Far from avoiding in dialogue objections, considerations and counter-examples that may be introduced, what is essential is to encourage them, whether one ends up altering one's position or whether one chooses to maintain it. Only thus can a decision or view be less blind and one-sided, and can it acquire a greater warrant. The goal should be an authentic, uncompelled consensus, not the pap of false agreement; and to reach such a consensus, healthy engagement in confrontation is necessary.

I saw at close quarters the man who, on reaching the premiership, became, with fatal consequences, the outstanding practitioner of false consensus. For Harold Wilson it was an art form and, one *apparatchik* praising another, caused Jim Callaghan at Wilson's memorial service to call on us to admire, above all, Wilson's skill as the party manager. It was indeed remarkable how Wilson, to avoid at all costs even acknowledging that he was facing antagonism, would, to disarm and placate an internal party opponent, deploy all his considerable intellectual powers to prove that even the most mutually exclusive objectives were not incompatible and would indeed often attempt to pursue all of them; and, as a consequence, usually did not properly achieve any of them. Elsewhere, in my 1973 book *Private Member*, I have written about Wilson's notorious Walter Mitty fantasies, his misplaced optimism, his dream that the outside environment was ever benevolent and never hostile, that no enemies need exist, that all could join in consensus, a stance he often endeavoured to maintain intact by having no one around him who disturbed his worry-free dream; no voice in his circle was to be heard murmuring that the emperor had no clothes. Although the aetiology of Blair's spurious consensus-seeking is to be distinguished from Wilson's, I became aware during the committee stages of the Matrimonial and Family Proceedings Bill of the parallels between Wilson's approach and that of this *arriviste*. An awareness of these parallels alerted me; this was no sweet, asexual, gentle Bambi, as the media was initially to depict Blair. Reconciling the irreconcilable, practising all the Wilsonian artifices of denying the existence of contradiction, insisting there was no difficulty in the lion lying down together with the lamb, may bemuse and comfort the credulous; but peddling such soothing political opiates can become a sinister occupation. In Blair's case it has led him to repudiate any hint of partisanship in Labour's policies, to affect that the tatty fabric of our society can be splendidly restored without raising taxes, without extending the powers of the state, without compulsorily taking back the nation's natural resources and public utilities into civic hands, and without any imposition upon what the presently privileged describe as their individual freedom.

Blair, in short, is the populist who, at a time when the incompetence and sleaze of governance has left many disenchanted with politics, panders to this widespread mood by seeking to de-politicise the Labour Party. He goes even further than Wilson, who proffered a magic solvent, a new technology, whose white heat would dissipate yesterday's struggles and conflicts, and precipitate an electoral coalescence, a Labour Party that would be the natural party of government. That goal does not satisfy Blair. Propelled by profound inner needs that are more significant even than his wish to take up heroic stands against those he knows are in retreat, he ceaselessly continues expanding the boundaries. His wish is to become the leader of a party above party, representing society as a whole; Labour, he told the 1995 Labour Party conference, was the one-nation party, a claim that comes perilously near to acclaiming the ideal of a one-party nation. It follows that those who demur, and would dare to mock this impossible and, within a democracy, sinister dream must be treated as cranks or outlaws; by the autumn of 1995 he was declaring in an *Observer* interview that 'those who fail to fall in' with his modernising project 'need their heads examined' and added an ominous comment, reminiscent of Soviet incarcerations of political opponents in mental hospitals, that in his view, although he was a politician not a psychiatrist, such opponents 'require not leadership but therapy'.

In the summer of 1995 the sage trade union leader John Edmonds had pleaded with Blair to desist and have 'a period of consolidation'. The plea fell on deaf ears. Blair told Edmonds's union conference that the process of 'reform' would never end. This process, which Edmonds described disparagingly as 'permanent revolution', is not simply a tactical manoeuvre to gain the support of more and more voters however diverse in reality their interests may be; it is, I believe, an irrational compulsive process which becomes Blair's temperament. But it can be a dangerous assault since our democracy is pinned up by adversarial party politics.

An assumption that one party, binding together all strands of opinion, can be representative of a society is a credo suitable only for an authoritarian state and is alien to British democracy. This is a lesson which I relearned in the first few minutes of my entry as an MP into the Palace of Westminster. On my arrival the attendant in the men's cloakroom pointed out to me the coat-hook assigned for my personal use. A loop of pink ribbon was tied around it, as around everyone else's hook. Intrigued, I questioned the flunkey, who told me, unsmilingly and with hauteur, that the loops were to hold the swords that must be deposited by MPs before they entered the Chamber. Evidently combativeness was traditionally expected, indeed demanded, from those entering the Chamber. But adversaries must confine themselves to verbal violence; and inside the Chamber each Member must know his defined territory, for it is not permitted, while speaking, to cross the thin red line woven into the carpet of the aisle which divides the two front benches, an aisle which itself is the length of two swords. Any Member whose foot does cross the line, if only by an inch, is immediately called to order by angry colleagues from all corners of the House. Such rituals and procedures should not be mocked; they are outward expressions of the belief that party divisions are essential to the working of our parliamentary democracy. We want no truck with round chambers – the plan of the building ensures that Government and Opposition face each other squarely; and there are no cross-benches in the Commons. Although in the present Parliament there are too many oafs who, colluding with the cameras, would reduce party politics to institutional paranoia, Disraeli's belief that 'without party parliamentary government is impossible' should be regarded by those who value parliamentary democracy as unchallengeable.

But those like Wilson and Blair who seek to define their

leadership not by their beliefs, which they prefer to remain suspended, but by proclaiming how representative they are of the whole nation, inevitably find the parameters set by our healthy tradition of party conflict intolerably constrictive; all of them attempt to escape from their dilemma in ways which can be strikingly similar. Recently in *The Times*, Matthew Parris, the unerring and perspicacious Parliamentary observer who has, as a former Conservative MP, the advantage of experience as participant as well as observer, was noting the parallels between Wilson and Blair which had prompted my own early misgivings.

Parris was struck that Blair, at Wilson's memorial service, chose to praise him by repeating the dead prime minister's words:

> The Labour Party is a moral crusade or it is nothing. Let, said Blair, that be his epitaph ... But, of course, Wilson's Labour Party was not a moral crusade. It was anything but. His career was many things, but never that. It was marked by his failure to become any sort of moral crusade. His enemies came to execrate (and his admirers to celebrate) the skill with which, time and again, issues of principle were sidelined, skirted or postponed.

Acquitting Blair, unlike Wilson, of any open attempt to celebrate his own rectitude, Parris, however, continued:

> But the language tells another story. Scan his abstract nouns and you will sniff a curious blend of pulpit and school assembly. The vocabulary is of trust and honour; of compassion, conviction, vocation; of humanity, integrity, community, morality, honesty and probity; of values, standards, faiths and beliefs. In the Commons he slips into the habit of implied superior virtue. With indignation just a shade too righteous and eyes just a mite too wide, he appeals to the heavens to be his judge.

The large, intangible claims and aspirations to which Parris finds Blair is wedded were already nascent when I found Blair sitting next to me in those early committee proceedings. Although the cautious, high-minded young man clearly found my approach too combative when I sought to amend or defend a clause in the Bill, he nevertheless was unpleasantly careful to avoid any direct confrontation with me. The most he did was, with a sweet smile on one occasion, to suggest 'with respect, that the Honourable Member for Torfaen had gone slightly over the top in some of his rhetoric'. In retrospect, now alerted to Blair's relationship with his father, Leo, I suspect some of his circumspection came from an inhibition to challenge someone bearing the commanding father's name; but at the time, and now, I find studied circumspection in the young unbecoming, not necessarily deferential or courteous. I concluded there was no danger of this man going 'over the top' to fight an enemy genuinely capable of retaliation. His later well-publicised 'battles' were to be bloodless charades: the abolition of Clause Four, all political initiates knew, involved a fake struggle since he was pushing against wide open doors; and in Blair's shabby failed conspiracy to neuter the Transport and General Workers' Union by replacing good Bill Morris with his own egregious stooge, he certainly kept his head down and left the going over the top to his lieutenants, who happily were outwitted by Morris when, to their consternation, he called a premature union election which left them in disarray. Such spurious 'heroic' stances were to become more explicit but they were not absent in Blair's early committee speeches. Observing and hearing him led me to conclude that his evasion of confrontation and his accompanying placatory skills would take him a long way in the Commons but not necessarily in the correct direction.

Exhibitionism: Do I Exist?

The theatricality, the overacting in speech and demeanour, from which Parris recoils had from the beginning already jarred on me. Grey politics, ill-designed, without drama or colour, is, of course, a poor thing; an emphatic declaration in dress and gesture can capture the attention of the unheeding. There was a time, indeed, when my waistcoats and garb, created by my designer wife, would, as I entered the House each Budget Day, capture the attention of television viewers and the readers of the national press. My gesture was not mere self-indulgent exhibitionism. It made a statement founded on the socialist principles of the artist-craftsman William Morris which as a boy I had learned from those wise elders who had permitted me to attend the proceedings of the Cardiff society bearing his name; a well-designed society should have well-designed accoutrements, buildings, furniture, fabrics and dress to be enjoyed by all. My act was in fact a defiance of the covert sumptuary laws maintained by those Tories who patronisingly believed that finery was for them and socialists should wear cloth caps. Of course my gesture shocked some, not least the puritanical *petit*

66

bourgeois Jim Callaghan, who, after my first Budget Day entry, priggishly told me my political career was ruined and that I had no future as an MP. My constituents thought otherwise; and so did a substantial section of the public, who, having focused upon my attire, were now much more ready to focus on my words, on my campaigns for social reforms. I do not therefore despise the controlled introduction of drama into politics; but form must match content. Theatre is one thing, theatricality, lacking wit, another.

Samuel Johnson, when told by the great Shakespearean actor David Garrick that every time he played Richard III he felt like a murderer, made the rejoinder: 'Then, Sir, you should be hanged.' Evidently in Garrick's performance there was no gap between the portrayal and the hunchback king. A great actor belongs totally to his part; but only too often one sees an actor observing and appreciating his own performance and, by his preening, by his estrangement from the assigned rôle, he leaves his audience no less estranged and unconvinced.

A politician faces a greater hazard, for his artificiality, if such is his condition, would be betrayed not only by his demeanour but, as Parris underlines, by his vocabulary. The politician uses – or, in these days of speechwriters, chooses – his own words; and these may subvert rather than corroborate his affirmation of genuineness. Even a good actor can be perceived as second-rate when provided with a shoddy script; and with the politician, the individual nouns, verbs, adjectives and adverbs he has chosen, even as much as the content of his speeches, can nullify his persuasions and leave his audience to categorise him as a phoney. Such an accusation may be attracted not only by an obvious B-feature ham actor like Reagan; the discerning may find more sophisticated appeals suspect.

Abstract nouns for which, as Parris has pointed out, Blair has a penchant can act as a shield, keeping complexities and painful realities at a distance. He ensures that nouns which possess an excessive resonance, likely to offend the politically timorous, are gutted. His wordplay is dextrous; by the use of a hyphen he seeks to bury socialism, telling his supporters: 'Once socialism is defined in this way – as social-ism – we can be liberated from our history and not chained by it.' And then, in turn, to placate suspicious traditionalists impatient with such decorous re-definitions, he introduced in May 1996 at the Welsh Labour Party conference a fresh phrase into New Labour's lexicon, one that could mask the incompatibility of consensus politics with fundamental change; the Labour Party, he told bemused delegates, was now 'the party of one-nation radicals'. Yet in all his various presentations one notes that he is like an actor who does not belong to his part; despite his attempts by overemphases to surmount the difficulty, he often repetitively uses an adjective or adverb to claim a condition which does not truly belong to him. He is forever claiming he 'passionately' believes, that he has 'passionate' convictions. Such declarations of passion are reminiscent of a wooing hero in a Victorian melodrama. In our public lives, as in our private lives, genuine commitment is not expressed, hand on heart, in adolescent protestation. Still, not babbling, waters run deep.

Blair so often flounders in the shallow but defined channel that divides the actor from the authentic politician. Nye Bevan, the exponent of Old Labour, well understood that distinction and had the strength to resist any tide tugging him towards an histrionic shore. He warned:

> Overprepared speeches rarely succeed. The audience in the theatre is radically different from that of a deliberative assembly or a political meeting. People go to the theatre in a mood to give themselves to the magic of illusion. They expect time and space and the constrictions of reality to be set aside in the service of theatrical conventions. They expect ... that the actors and actresses should speak their lines with clarity of diction because they are fundamentally mimes subordi-nated to their parts in the performance ... the political speaker is in an entirely different category.

But Blair does not fall into an entirely different category; it can certainly be pleaded in mitigation that he is living in the world of the autocue, and the spontaneity which Bevan demanded of the politician is no longer possible, but I do not think the content, manner and delivery of his set speeches can be explained solely in terms of modern technology. His personal history tells us otherwise. He has always been attracted to the stage, even as were his music-hall dancer and occasional actress grandmother, and his Pierrot-performing and straight actor grandfather. Singing in the choir of his prep school, standing as the Conservative candidate at 13 in the school's mock election, playing at his public school at 15 the part of Mark Antony in *Julius Caesar*, and then the lead in R C Sherriff's World War I drama *Journey's End* while singing tenor in Mozart pieces at school concerts, he was soon at Oxford to become a prominent member of the troupe in St John's College revues and lead singer in one rock band while playing in another. He left Oxford untutored in politics but not in stagecraft; in his present performance there are far more than vestigial traces of the extracurricular qualifications he acquired as an undergraduate.

In a quest to identify the particular and distinctive qualities which have led to Blair's present dominance, it would not necessarily be of assistance simply to remark that he has been stage-struck for, among politicians, exhibitionism is a generic condition; indeed, it is a qualification required in the CV of any budding politician. No MP is a shrinking violet; but Blair's persistent display of his mimetic talents, whether playing Shakespeare, in St John's revues, or in public impersonations of Mick Jagger, reveals, even for a politician, exhibitionism in an unusually undisguised and exotic form.

When exhibitionism becomes overt, when it shows itself in the behaviour of the pathetic 'flashers' for whom I used to plead in magistrates' courts, or when it becomes obtrusive in unpleasantly histrionic behaviour, it tells of a failure to transmute the narcissism which is the endowment of all of us in our earliest years. The ultimate test is to be found in our capacity, as we grow into adulthood, to transmute our original feelings of grandiosity, of omnipotence, of narcissism unlimited, into a self-esteem and self-confidence which can show themselves as a genuine concern for others as well as ourselves. For that transmutation to take place successfully, the psychoanalysts tell us, our first carers must not regard our earliest narcissistic traits as arrogant and self-serving; as demands to be fiercely denied. Instead, they should acknowledge them joyfully and with empathy until the soothed baby – no longer compelled to test his power to command – weans himself away from the need for total narcissistic gratification, gains self-confidence and, in the end, obtains his self-gratification and esteem from his own activity and creativity. But when the child's self-assertive presence is not adequately responded to by the mother, then the narcissistic injury thus inflicted never heals; in adulthood the prohibited exhibitionism, raw and untreated, exudes, at its worst, criminal perversion and, at its best, less antisocial responses.

But the failure of a babe to receive the corroboration of his healthy narcissism always leaves him bereft, and can lead to him being uncertain of his very existence. Indeed, latter-day psychoanalysts define exhibitionism as a manic defence against loss of identity: 'I must be real because I'm being looked at.' I have seen this syndrome dramatically presented when meeting famed actors and actresses and finding them empty, vapid and colourless but who become miraculously alive when on stage and given an identity they themselves lack.

And, of course, although usually in milder form, the same signs of early deprivation of corroboration abound among politicians; forever they clamour for attention. There are some optimistic psychiatrists who would seek to persuade us that the psycho-pathology of the politician, thus expressed, is not important; what is important is the creative use they make of their psycho-pathology. And it has to be conceded that sometimes their flow of provocations, ideas and manifestos, giving them the attention and thus the comforting confirmation of their own reality, results in net gains for the nation. Too often, however, the consequences are less than benign; and certainly that is how I would categorise the consequences that come from Blair's existentialist waverings. As actor or performer doubtless he brought pleasure. His small step from stage to political platform in search of identity may have assisted him in his personal resolution, but it has left my Labour Party shorn; he has taken away the identity of Labour and reshaped it to suit his own psychological measurements. This operation is described by his supporters as 'reform'; I call it theft.

We can note the exhibitionist symptoms of unassuaged infantile narcissism when a politician is forever belatedly seeking an identity corroboration denied to him as a babe. Although in the generality we can rest upon the clinical findings of the paediatricians and psychoanalysts who affirm the source of such restlessness lies in the absence of 'good enough mothering', perforce, evidentially, there are grave difficulties in establishing the fact in the particular; but although these obstacles necessitate caution, we should not be deterred when the exhibitionism of the individual politician is so florid and various that it is undeniable that it has stamped upon it all the hallmarks delineated by the clinicians.

And we should be quizzical when such politicians, finding it too painful to accept that they received anything but unstinting, exclusive love and care from their mothers, indulge in idealisations of their mothers.

Predictably, Blair's overpliant biographer tells us how Blair 'adored' his mother, the 'down to earth' daughter of a Glasgow butcher, and how, in turn, we are informed: 'It was absolutely clear she doted on Tony.' She may have provided him with an audience but when she died, tragically early, Blair's declared handling of his grief does not present a picture of a satiated man who felt he had received adequate recognition from his mother. No stillness appears in his mourning. All of us pass through a kaleidoscope of emotions on the death of a parent, but with Blair, his odd dominant response was to use the occasion in an extraordinary self-directive manner. He has said that the death 'strangely galvanised him'. He converted the death into a spur to drive himself on, frenetically, to achieve rapidly his narcissistic satisfactions: 'I think the death of someone very close to you does act as a spur to you, because as well as your grief for the person your own mortality comes home to you. And you suddenly realise – which often you don't as a young person – that life is finite, so if you want to get things done you had better get a move on.' Getting 'a move on' immediately manifested itself, despite his previous lack of interest in politics, in his joining the Labour Party; to Blair 'moving on' and 'moving up' carried the same meaning.

One of Blair's aides has quipped that when travelling in a car with Blair the item that gets most used is the passenger's vanity mirror; the mirror-gazing is not to be dismissed as mere vanity. Psychoanalysts, particularly those who are followers of Heinz Kohut, who made many emendations to classic Freudian theory, stress that for a healthy self to develop, to gain cohesion and balance, the babe requires adequate satisfaction of what they call 'mirroring' needs. These are the babe's needs to feel affirmed, confirmed, recognised, to feel accepted and appreciated – especially when he displays himself. If those needs are unsatisfied, mirror-gazing in adulthood is a belated attempt to obtain the reassurance that he is there, whole and in one piece. These days, this fear of dissolution, which was formerly overcome by many a politician in the confirmatory audience response at public meetings, is warded off by television. Thanks to the recording video, a politician can now indulge his exhibitionism on television and then, subsequently, see himself on the screen. The MP guards his videotapes of himself jealously; they have freed him from having to find someone else to look at him and confirm that his identity has not gone missing.

The technology is new but not the phenomenon. I can recall, long before I came into the Commons, a meeting which I chaired in a Cardiff cinema addressed by the then Foreign Secretary, Herbert Morrison, grandfather of Blair's principal aide, Peter Mandelson. Despite the attraction of being outdoors on a hot

Sunday afternoon, the meeting was packed and, in that pre-air-conditioning era, the hall became uncomfortably warm. As I opened the proceedings I was aware of the understandable listlessness of the audience, and I hoped the inquisitiveness which had brought them to see and hear the Foreign Secretary would overcome their somnolence. It was not to be. For an hour Morrison pompously read his prepared Foreign Office brief, cautiously never departing from the text; the audience wilted, and the applause when Morrison eventually concluded was so muted that even Morrison's conceit could not sustain him. He grumpily accompanied me to the small dinner party that had been arranged at the home of a supporter. After the first course, as our proud hostess was carrying in her *pièce de résistance*, Morrison abruptly commanded the service and eating to cease; he was aware, as we were not, that lengthy recorded excerpts of his speech were to be given on the wireless, and on his order one of his officials placed a radio on the dinner table and once again we were subjected to his verbal torture. As the broadcast speech droned on, we drooped in despair and embarrassment but Morrison's moroseness left him and he became the famed chirpy Cockney. Even more than most politicians, he was in love with his own voice; and thus supported, while we disconsolately ate our now cold fare, he pronounced the evening a great success. Indeed, so pleased was he with himself, and thus with me, that the following day he told regional officers of the party that they should endeavour to find a South Wales seat for me. His good opinion of me was not to last long; when I did reach the Commons, in a xenophobic tirade he endeavoured to smear left-wing MPs by pointing out we were a bunch who, from A to Z, from Abse to Zilliacus, with Mikardo in the middle, had doubtful origins. Given his prejudices, or perhaps because of them, it was ironic that his daughter married the well-liked advertising manager of the *Jewish Chronicle*.

But on that occasion, when Morrison used his recorded voice to gain the approbation denied to him by his audience, his behaviour was but a caricature of the technique we all use when we are, literally, uncertain of ourselves. In the dark, feeling alone, we ward off the threats we fear from without and within by humming or whistling to ourselves; total silence can de-personalise us. Whistling in the dark is not a practice confined to politicians; but one of the sources of their notorious loquacity, like their gregariousness, is their particular incapacity to be alone; the jibe that they like their own voices too much is justified, but there is a plaintive plea lurking behind all their prolix outpourings. Respond to us, applaud us, tell us we are here; we fear our dissolution; give us not only your vote but cheer us, and so, by your voices, give us the corroboration that we did not receive as babes in our mothers' arms.

Donald Winnicott, the paediatrician whose work has so influenced contemporary English psychoanalysis, has spelled out the origins of this incapacity to relish solitude, this extraordinary need always to have the presence of others with whom one can communicate. Incapacity to be alone originates, Winnicott tells us, with the infant's experience of being alone in the presence of his mother. If the child's immediate needs have been satisfied, if he has received warmth, physical contact and food, and if the babe sees the approving mirroring gleam in the mother's eye, when there is no further need for the mother to be concerned with immediately providing anything more, nor any need for the babe to be looking immediately to the mother for everything, then, at such moments, there is a blissful silence. The relatedness between mother and child, Winnicott tells us, is the basis of the capacity to be alone: 'The paradox of the capacity to be alone is based on the experience of being alone in the presence of someone and without a sufficiency of this experience the capacity to be alone cannot be developed.'

So many of our compulsively gregarious politicians suffer from, and make us suffer for, their insufficiency of that experience; and, since a prerequisite to enjoying that experience is to have the blessing of a succouring empathic mother who, with love, tends and feeds the child, it unsurprisingly follows we find so many politicians who fall into the category described, 70 years ago, as 'oral character types' by Karl Abraham, the man regarded by British Kleinian analysts as their founding father. Abraham traced the link between the babe who had received inadequate gratification by way of sucking and the incessant adult talker. In infancy all of us have an intense pleasure in the act of sucking, but Abraham insisted that this pleasure was not to be ascribed entirely to the process of taking food but that it is conditioned in a high degree by the significance of the mother as an erotogenic zone; some of that early enjoyed erotic activity finds a place in the kissing of adult lovers, but such is our oral erotic endowment that this outlet is insufficient to deplete its supply. The primitive form of obtaining pleasure through sucking has to persist in all sorts of disguises during the whole of our lives, and Abraham thought that certain traits of character can be traced back to singular displacements, particularly by those feeling orally deprived:

> Their longing to seek gratification by way of sucking has changed to a need to *give* by way of the mouth, so that we find in them, besides a permanent longing to obtain everything, a constant need to communicate themselves orally to other people. This results in an obstinate urge to talk, connected in most cases with a feeling of overflowing. Persons of this kind have the impression that their fund of thought is inexhaustible, and they ascribe a special power of some unusual value to what they say.

For 30 years, daily, in the great talking-shop of Westminster, I found clinical material which all too chasteningly illustrated Abraham's theory. The most insufferable confirmation came from Harold Wilson. In public he had no reputation for brevity and many of his speeches were ruined by their longevity; his book rendering his account of his governments stands witness to his disregard for economical presentation. But he was no less unendurable in private. On not a few occasions, arriving late in the Members' dining-room and finding all the smaller tables occupied, I fled the House to an outside restaurant rather than sit at one of the vacant places at the large table over which Wilson presided; there, his rôle as leader of the party meant he commanded the deference which enabled him to talk without interruption – and he would take advantage of his position.

When Wilson spoke to you, it was not a rapport that was being established; rather, you felt he was relating to you in the only way open to him, by way of oral discharge. And not content to leave his words to be spoken once, a disproportionate amount of his conversation would be spent on what he had recently said to the women of Bootle or the Trades Council at Llanelli, and how large were his audiences, and how well they responded. And he would recall unimportant meetings of long ago with an astonishing wealth of detail, savouring them yet again as would an aged man recalling the *affaires* of his youth. If he stopped his compulsive talking, you wondered if he would disappear into thin air. Wilson revealed all the inner apprehensions of the incessant talker which Logan Pearsall Smith, the famed literary critic, once sensitively described: 'It is the dread of something happening, something unknown and dreadful, that makes us do anything to keep the flicker of talk from dying out.'

But garrulousness is a vulgar stratagem to ward off fears of dissolution; I have observed, when sharing platforms with some sophisticated politicians, auditory ruses that are much more inventive. James Griffiths, the architect of our National Insurance scheme, as his speeches advanced and his decidedly chapel oratory held his audience, while speaking, would close his eyes as if in a trance, and Roy Jenkins sometimes, if not so emphatically, can similarly shut his eyes. These gestures are not to be dismissed as mere mannerisms. By having the audience look at you while simultaneously listening to yourself, you have the double assurance of your own presence, of your own reality. You can obtain the applause of the audience while at the same time lulling yourself into security by listening to your own lullabies, the ones you did not receive but wanted when clasped in your mother's arms. The gesture, of course, can be interpreted as an attempt to blind yourself to painful truths, past and present, internal and external; but the quiddity of the eye movement is the protection it affords against disintegration. It has not been part of the protective armoury of Blair; he has used another technique to reach the same ends. He opens his eyes wide, too wide, sees his admiring audience and then, in song, Mozart or rock, has obtained his listeners' approval while having the solace of hearing himself. He is thus more shameless in his exhibitionism, but doubtless his need is greater.

The Outsiders: Leo and Tony

The very desperation of Blair's need for corroboration leaves one unconvinced, despite all the inferential evidence that can be marshalled, that the sole source of this hunger for external approbation is to be found in his unassuaged infantile narcissism. Moving at an extraordinary pace, unencumbered by any serious political baggage, en route from earliest infancy to Downing Street, what else, one wonders, has spurred on this young man? One incitement is his place within the family constellation which ensured he would not lack for sibling rivalry. Second sons, forever attempting to elbow their way to the front, striving to obtain the priority their birth day has denied them, have often been remarked upon in the Labour movement, where second sons with able elder brothers have, from Stafford Cripps and Harold Laski to Tony Benn, frequently provided significant leadership. The dynamism behind sibling rivalry can be benign or destructive, and sometimes both, and its force should not be underestimated politically in a family where the resources of the mother-provider are meagre and the brothers begin their lives fighting over small morsels of love and recognition. The wish to blaze high in the family firmament is effortlessly displaced in adult life to the political party whose members, as part of its trades union inheritance, so recently, until sanitised by Blair and his kind, addressed each other as 'Brother'.

And does yet another incitement to be way out front come from the particular circumstances of his Scottish origins? Or is he, as some of his Scottish colleagues would have us believe, *déraciné*, the grandson of the English land-owning class, educated at Scotland's Eton and at Oxford, suitably representing an English seat? Those questions are certainly politically relevant but to obtain answers we should focus not upon his formal schooling, but upon his upbringing within a family dominated by a politically ambitious father. It is true that, by chance, Tony's father, Leo, was brought up in Scotland, but it is an exploration of the geography of Leo Blair's mind, not the venue of his first home, that provides us with some of the answers we are seeking.

Glib, too glib, in his oft-repeated affirmations of family values, Blair has told of his good fortune in coming from a 'very closely knit family', and certainly he remains tied to a father who is a case study of the outsider striving to become the insider. Blair's sympathetic biographer has described Leo as 'a walking advertisement for social mobility'; he was the illegitimate son of the daughter of a wealthy land-owning family in West Sussex and was dumped upon a Clydeside shipyard rigger and his wife, to be brought up in a tenement in near-poverty, and forced to leave school at 14 in order to find work. His predicament and the resentment of the class from which his mother sprang made Blair's father an active communist but the war gave the outsider the opportunity to get on to the inside track. He left behind his secretaryship of the Scottish Young Communist League and in the army took another route; he rejoined the class from which he had been expelled. He rose from being a private to become a major and in the post-war world became one of the leading Tories in the North-East and, but for the cruel misfortune of suffering a severe stroke, it is likely he would have become the

MP for Hexham. He had moved a long way from the Govan, and intends to keep it that way. Forever determined to belong to the establishment which now, thanks to his son, will soon be New Labour, he has effortlessly glided from the Conservative Party to join New Labour. With him as an exemplar, his son continues to thrive on political lability.

If he had entered the House as a Conservative MP, Leo Blair would have been one of those who come from the 'outer margins' and whom Isaiah Berlin has contrasted with those born within the solid security of the dominant settled society and who look upon it as their natural home. Berlin notes the fiery vision, noble or degraded, of the outsiders: Napoleon from Corsica; Gambetta from the southern borderlands; the Austrian Hitler; and Theodor Herzl and Trotsky from the outer rim of the assimilated edges of the Jewish world. Berlin could certainly have added to his list the Welsh Lloyd George, the most notable outsider since Disraeli to attain the premiership. Berlin too could have underlined his contentions by pointing out that Napoleon, born in Corsica of Italian origin, had an imperfect knowledge of French; that Garibaldi, born in Nice, a French citizen, spoke clumsy Italian; and that Herzl, a secular Western European Jew, found the majority of his followers among East European Jews whose language, Yiddish, he hardly knew. Given the dreams, some misshapen, some idealistic, of these outsider leaders, Berlin concludes that, in contrast, the insider leaders 'tend to have a stronger sense of social reality, to see public life in reasonably just perspective, without the need to escape into political fantasy or romantic inventions'.

Tony Blair, unconvincingly, seeks to explain and justify his father's trajectory in quite different terms; he presents him, speciously, as a 'gut Conservative' chafing against the restrictions imposed upon him by the collective society and does him the serious injustice of comparing him with Norman Tebbit, a man regarded by many as an exponent of gutter politics. But if we leave fiction for fact, then the strivings of the outsider and ersatz Scot, Leo Blair, no Essex man, are seen to be of the type explicated by Isaiah Berlin when writing of outsiders' craving for recognition:

> It is an effort to escape from the weakness and humiliation of a depressed or wounded social group by identifying oneself with some other group or movement that is free from the defects of one's original condition; consisting in an attempt to acquire a new personality, and that which goes with it, a new set of clothing, a new set of values, habits, new armour which does not press upon the old wounds, on the old scars left by the chains one wore as a slave.

When we note the swing of Leo Blair from Young Communist to High Tory, we wonder how apposite to him are Berlin's comments on those, suffering discrimination, who start their lives feeling they are excluded from participation in the governance of the community:

> They are liable to develop either exaggerated resentment of, or contempt for, the dominant majority, or else overintense admiration or indeed worship for it, or, at times, a combination of the two which leads both to unusual insights and – born of overwrought sensibilities – a neurotic distortion of the facts.

But for the terrible fate of suffering a stroke at 40, Leo Blair would undoubtedly have become an insider, feeling confident that he had become part of the 'dominant majority', a Tory MP with the drive and intelligence to become a minister. As it was, his son was to be brought up in a home where the stricken father, intensely buttoned up about his origins, had nearly, but not quite, rid himself of his past and nearly, but not quite, obtained the recognition which would have meant that he had achieved what he most wanted: to belong, to cancel out his rejection and his illegitimacy. How did that enforced limbo, physical and psychological, endured by Leo, impinge upon his young son – and with what ultimate political consequence?

The influence of Leo Blair upon his son is, in some respects, blatant, most obviously in the young Tony's fledgeling politics. The boy in his earliest years was immersed in Tory politics, with his father as chairman of the Durham Conservative Association receiving into his home many of the leading Conservatives passing through the North-East; and, after his father's enforced retirement, his son remained loyally and firmly attached to the doctrines in which he had been reared. His rôle as a would-be Tory candidate at 13 in his school's mock elections shows not only his political precocity but, more significantly, the continuing strength of his father's influence. I know how family influences had shaped my politics when, at the same age as young Tony, I stood as a Labour candidate in a mock election held at my valiant run-down secondary school, and I wryly recall my presumptuousness in writing to the then leader of the Labour Party, George Lansbury, asking him for a letter of support – which brought back a sensitive and warm commendation which, well passed round the school, ensured my victory. And even as the Welsh socialist pacifist tradition within my family shaped my boyhood politics, so did the influence of his family bear down upon the young Tony as he strove to emulate his father. The impress of my early family conditioning remains deeply embossed upon my political thought; and, similarly, if less unequivocally, does the impress of Leo Blair upon the political stances of his son.

· But more subtle, yet no less pervasive, paternal influences appear to have been at work. All feelings of rejection, of not belonging, which Leo Blair had so courageously attempted, with partial success, to overcome, would surely have been reactivated as once again he found himself within a hostile environment, one in which a cruel and debilitating stroke had left him as a baby, for years speechless and utterly dependent. The man who had so courageously battled to break out from an outer wilderness found himself expelled from the centrality of his political life and reduced to a peripheral rôle even within the family he had commanded. Tony Blair was thus brought up in a home overcast by the estrangement of his father, a man who by his own efforts had become in the post-war years a successful academic lawyer, and then, at 40, was tragically fated to be reduced, by his physical condition, to being once again an outcast even as he had been as an illegitimate child. Those feelings of Leo Blair, of not belonging, of alienation, have been picked up, as the record shows, by his son. Repeatedly, surveying Blair's passage through his public school, university and party, one's attention is arrested by the incapacity of this good-looking, intelligent and seemingly socially fluent individual to feel, despite his advantages, at home within the institutions which house him; sometimes, indeed, so acute is his discomfort that he cannot forbear not to make it public.

When I have spoken to some of his contemporaries at the Durham Cathedral Choristers' Preparatory School, their recall always emphasises his non-participation, outside the organised school games, in the play of the kids in nearby open spaces; he was often ferried in from the nearby village of executive houses, where he lived, by his father – remembered as a stern, forbidding figure – and then, after school, Blair returned home direct. He was a 'good boy', average in his studies, but doing well in scripture and thus conforming to the religiosity that pervaded the all-male establishment and was felt, at least by some of the choirboy pupils, as sickly and tinged by a vague eroticism. He is also remembered at the school by his ever-present smile directed towards the teachers, a smile which then was successfully used to deflect any potential hostility and which now he still so notoriously deploys, and which indeed has become his political trade-mark; and with his Canon headmaster he ingratiated himself, for side by side they fervently prayed together.

As biographer, Jon Sopel has evidently been overpersuaded that Tony Blair was therefore very much at home at the prep school. A closer scrutiny of the facts and the recall of some of his contemporaries more strongly suggest a façade, a priggish adaptation by a stress-loaded boy, which accommodated to the environment but which failed to be sustained when he left the prep school for the rigours of Fettes public school.

At Fettes, often called 'Eton in a kilt', Blair would have encountered the highly disciplined and structured environment of an old-fashioned and rigid public school. Doubtless many boys found it tough, but few would so fail to adapt to its group ethos. Blair packed his bags and, literally, ran away; it needed all his father's persuasions for him to be taken back. Only in fantasy, in the school drama productions, could he find himself, and the only extant commendation of Blair at Fettes appears to be the comment, after he had appeared in a school play, in the school magazine that the college had been 'very fortunate in having so experienced an actor as Blair for the central figure'. Whether his continuing histrionic ability is fortunate for the Labour Party is another matter.

As for Oxford, his alienation there is, on the surface, quite extraordinary. He has told his biographer that, 'looking back', he felt he 'never really belonged to Oxford'. Absurdly patronisingly and, given his second-class degree, defensively, he says: 'Oxford, far from being intellectually invigorating, is actually rather stifling. There was very little room for fresh or original thought ... all the time I was at Oxford I felt an outsider.' When in the past I visited Oxford to speak to student societies, I found youngsters from comprehensive schools in my constituency, sons of miners or steel-workers, who under-standably felt lost in the ancient university. But why should the public school boy, coming from an upper-middle-class family, good-looking, with a string of undergraduate girlfriends, 'enjoying himself ', he says, performing in revues, in sketches and playing music, be so wretchedly afflicted with anomie? The cause is not to be found in Oxford or in any other external circumstances of his undergraduate days; it was older and more deep-seated. Tony Blair carried within him the depression and grief in which, as a member of Leo Blair's family, he had, as a boy, been engulfed.

Feeling the outsider in Oxford was part of Blair's personal

travail; but carrying that estrangement into the Labour Party has made the personal problem a public one, for he could no more 'belong', in the full sense that Nye Bevan stressed, to the Labour Party than he could to his schools and Oxford. In July 1995, after the special conference called to gut Clause Four of Labour's constitution, he made a comment which, even as he made it, astonished him as much as his *Guardian* interviewer; he announced that the whole process of effecting the change had been an education for him, belatedly introducing him to the Labour Party: 'I know my Labour Party very well now. It may be a strange thing to say but before I became leader I did not.'

It may be 'strange' to him but, given his particular psychic disablement, and the consequent repetitive pattern of his tenuous relationship with the institutions he has joined, it is not strange to me; but it is offensive, as it is to others within my dwindling generation of Old Labour. Our entry into, and our understanding of, our party did not come by way of some blinding Damascus revelation; nor did we qualify for our membership by filling in an application form in a glossy magazine. My experience is not atypical even if, as has been reported, in standing as a candidate 17 times in local and national elections, I have been the standard-bearer for Labour more times than anyone now alive, and even although, as becomes a Labour veteran, I have been arrested and for a very short while imprisoned because of my political activities; some such experiences, victimisation in the workshop, appalling exploitation in mine or factory, prolonged periods of unemployment and poverty, shaped most of the political activists of Old Labour. Displaying the same hubris towards them as he has towards his old university, in the same interview in which he revelled in his efforts to create Labour in his own blemished image, the young politician patronisingly added: 'The Labour Party is much nicer than it looks. Labour often looks as if it is about to engage in class war but in fact it is full of basically rather decent and honest people.' Unsurprisingly, vexed by his presumptuousness, some traditional supporters accuse him of 'betrayal'. They are in error. When the notorious alienated spy Kim Philby was stigmatised as a betrayer, he protested: 'To betray you must first belong.' Tony Blair could indeed be granted the same defence.

Disavowals

All of us, to a greater or lesser extent, seek to blot out our painful experiences, to disavow past fearsome or humiliating events in our lives. But the defence mechanism of denial is defective; it is liable to backfire. Our refusal to acknowledge the existence of our past agonies guarantees that, slyly, they will return in disguised forms, and often will demand a ransom from us for daring to ignore them. Our past pains and fears will never be tempered unless we face them.

Any overview of Blair's personal and political life reveals a man who depends upon denial as a principal weapon in his psychic armoury; predictably, this leaves him, as man and politician, vulnerable. Freud uses the term 'disavowal', *Verleugnung*, in the specific sense of a mode of thinking which consists of a refusal to recognise the reality of a traumatic perception. With Blair, disavowals of that quality abound. They are to be seen in his descriptions of his relationships with his mother, his father, his school and university, and in his account of his early life within the Blair family.

By idealisation of his mother, he denies any emotional

deprivation he may have felt in her arms. That judgement, thus baldly stated, has, it is immediately conceded, been reached only inferentially, by linking his marked exhibitionism to unassuaged narcissism, to a failure to have received, initially, sufficient loving corroboration; no other explanation seems to be available. And certainly such little as has been made known of his mother does not subvert that judgement.

Hazel Blair came out of a harsh, austere climate, that of the conservative Protestant farming community of the borderlands of Ulster. Blair's overgenerous biographer Jon Sopel, who received much aid and time from him and from his office staff, has recited a list of her virtues. He tells us that she was a 'practical', 'down to earth', 'shy' woman who reared her family with 'stoicism' and instilled into her children a 'sense of duty'. One is left feeling admiration for a woman who clearly met family adversity with resource and courage, but the choice of words in the eulogy is discouraging; it bears an uncomfortably close resemblance to the encoded masking vocabulary found in many an obituary notice. 'Shy' could mean uncommunicative, withdrawn, 'practical' could mean non-academic and perhaps rather dull, and 'down to earth' suggests unimaginativeness – all the qualities one would associate with a dutiful but unempathic mother. Blair himself, when recounting her main attribute, uses a noun which conveys a hard adamantine quality: she was the 'cement' that kept the family together.

Blair's use of the mechanism of denial is more explicitly revealed in the turmoil of his schooldays. Sopel has concluded that Blair 'at Fettes College found himself in a completely alien world' but does not offer any explanation why Blair, the son of a professional man, should be at odds with a school that was not peopled by lairds but by the sons of Edinburgh's merchant classes. Nevertheless, despite this alienation, and despite the rigours of the highly disciplined and oppressively structured environment imposed upon him, and despite the humiliations of the fag system, of which 'aspect of his school life he displays a marked reluctance to speak', Blair tells Sopel that 'for all the pettiness of Fettes' he came 'eventually to enjoy his time there'. The travails of his schooldays are distanced, almost totally denied, as his recollections dwell upon the comforting escape to fantasy in the school theatricals.

And in Oxford his flight from the predicaments of his inner loneliness as an 'outsider' took on a manic quality. Psychoanalysts define denial of psychical reality as a manifest-ation of a manic defence; it consists of denying the inner significance of experience, and in particular of depressive feelings. His biographer is forced to acknowledge that 'for all the fun of wine, women and song', Blair was 'restless' at Oxford. The biographer overstates the fun and underrates the significance of the so-called restlessness. Blair was attempting to cope not with unease but with dis-ease.

Almost frenetically he flung himself into the social whirl of undergraduate societies like the Archery Club, which had nothing to do with archery and everything to do with the affectation that its members were latter-day characters out of *Brideshead Revisited* having a 'good time' drinking at dinner parties which would be concluded by throwing champagne glasses out of the window. And thus Blair 'enjoyed' himself, dressing up on and off the stage in bizarre styles, sporting what he believed were trendy clothes, a vile synthetic skin coat or a curious black coat with well-displayed red lining. With his hair halfway down his back accompanied by a severe fringe, his father going to collect him from Oxford literally did not recognise his own son; and he would have been more taken aback if he had seen him wearing in his revue or rock-band appearances a hoop-necked, trumpet-sleeved T-shirt 'which stopped just beneath the ribcage, leaving a large acreage of rippling bare torso and beyond that there were the obligatory purple loons, topped off by Cuban-heeled cowboy boots'.

But for one factor, it would be priggish and irrelevant to comment on Blair's undergraduate behaviour. Many of the undergraduates, particularly those from public schools, burst out of their earlier shelterings and containments in similar fashion, and I noted at that time how prolonged and delayed was their adolescence compared with working-class young men, often married with a child, employed in the factories in my constituency. Given, however, the unconvincing explanations by Blair, telling us why he never in any way participated in the Union or the political societies of the university, his immaturity at Oxford is a legitimate subject for comment.

He found, he says, the activities of the Labour Club a 'complete turn-off ... I could not be bothered with that. I've always had a fairly practical turn of mind and student politics at Oxford never seemed very practical. Instead I generally enjoyed myself performing in revues, sketches ...' He 'loathed the falseness and pretentiousness and wanted no part in the affectations of would-be prime ministers'. These muddled rationalisations, with all their *non sequiturs*, telling how the 'practical' man preferred the falseness of the footlights to politics, would be bewildering unless we understand that here the adult Blair is masking the predicaments of young Blair at Oxford. There, as described by a much older fellow-student, an ordained priest who influenced Blair, he was a 'lost soul'. 'I think his life kind of lacked purpose and direction. Beyond getting a degree I don't think he knew what he was doing at Oxford, and I think he felt unsatisfied.'

If indeed his extraordinary claim that he was too practical to join in student politics had any substance, then he could have followed the example of not a few Oxbridge students who escaped the confines of the student societies and endeavoured to enter the real world by joining the local branch of the Labour Party. I often encountered such students during the short time that Robert Davies was the Labour MP for Cambridge – a man with whom, after he came into the Commons from a distinguished service on the local authority, I formed a friendship. Rigid, ideological but scrupulous, his rectitude was a personal disaster. Accustomed to need and to obtain, as can often occur in local government, speedy and useful results, he found himself on the back benches lacking function and, in an ineffectual limbo, despising the compromises of the 1966 government and those indigenous to Harold Wilson's temperament, he bravely, but desperately and fatally, hurled himself at the institution. In vain I counselled him to cultivate more detachment; but his fury and impatience with the political charades, the half-truths and evasions of Westminster, dangerously blew back upon him. Still in his 40s, after 15 months as an MP, this gifted man died of his honesty and the House of Commons. But during the time that he was in the Commons I sometimes accompanied him, at his request, to speak to his constituency party and there I found Cambridge students receiving tutorship from him and guidance from adult working-class fellow-party members, unavailable to them in the student societies.

If, similarly, Blair, too fastidious to participate in the politics of his fellow-students, had joined the Labour Party, he would undoubtedly have been exposed to some of the realities of the outside world. It would have introduced him to those in the local party from the Oxford working-class of Cowley and to those in the car plant there which, at the time of Blair's sojourn in Oxford, was a hotbed of political activism; and he might then have understood, through his contact with the trade union delegates on the management committee of the Oxford party, the intimacy existing between the Labour Party and the trade union movement and how the federal nature of the party, which in 1995 it was discovered he clandestinely was seeking to dismember, was its very lifeblood.

And if it was not that he was engaged in a flight from, and not a fight against, his alienation, the 'lost soul' could have found the 'communality' about which he forever prattles in the trade union branches where, tacitly, it is practised. I had found it there before the war when, as a teenager employed in a factory doing work, like Blair's father and so many of his and my generation, which denied our potential, I joined the Transport and General Workers' Union. When, with the opportunities made available to ex-servicemen in the post-war world, I became a solicitor, one of my greatest professional satisfactions was my capacity to repay my indebtedness to my union by giving its members legal aid and advice. The 'brothers' should not be mocked. Inside branches of the unions and the lodges of the miners there can come into existence loyalties and support of a rare quality; but their bonding has been formed not according to some fanciful theories but in struggle, and their allegiance of one to another has sprung out of conflict and confrontation.

Blair's notions of communality, however, come from a totally different source. In the latter days of his undergraduate life, he came under the influence of his friend Peter Thomson, the 36-year-old ordained priest who, as a mature student, was studying theology and whom Blair found 'spellbinding'; the spell never seems to have broken, for in 1995 Blair took his family across the world to spend his Christmas at Thomson's Merrijig home in the backwoods of Australia and there enticed him to return to Britain. Disinterested in the heavens since leaving behind his cathedral prep school prayers, under Thomson's influence once again the bewildered young man got into religion and became confirmed. He pursued it with all the enthusiasm of a novitiate and soon the priest had led him to the works of John Macmurray, which totally 'fascinated' him and which he now says are central to his political thinking; that is a claim which requires scrutiny.

Blair's biographer says Macmurray was 'an obscure Scottish philosopher'. He was certainly not obscure to me; 35 years before the young Blair trekked to Scotland from Oxford in the hope of sitting at the feet of his elderly guru, I had, at the same age as Blair, listened to him lecture, but the professor of moral philosophy did not make the same overwhelming impression on me as he did on Blair. I recall him, a man as short as I was and no less loquacious, lecturing on dialectical materialism and, in conciliatory tones, seeking to accommodate Christianity to Marxism; even as a 20-year-old socialist, I found his ecumenical expositions strained but, of course, politically welcome. The Macmurray that Blair encountered, however, was a man who had long since ceased to make his gentle, political forays; indeed, in his later book, the one specifically named by Blair as his guidebook, the earlier neo-Marxist essays are not listed amongst his previous publications.

Blair most certainly would not have obtained from Macmurray any encouragement to seek any political answers to the woes of the human predicament. On the contrary, the late works of Macmurray that Blair was reading mocked politics and politicians; community, Macmurray insisted, was to be found in religion, and politics were to be eschewed:

> If we track the state to its lair, what shall we find? Merely a collection of overworked and worried gentlemen, not at all unlike ourselves, doing their best to keep the machinery of government working as well as may be, and hard put to it to keep up appearances. They are, like ourselves, subject to the illusion of power. If we expect them to work miracles, we flatter them, and tempt them to think they are supermen ... Those of them who are wise enough to know their limitations, and to be immune to the gross adulation of their fellows, will resign; and government will be carried on only by megalomaniacs.

Blair's claim in 1994 that at Oxford Macmurray had led him to see the 'coincidence between the philosophical theory of Christianity and left-of-centre politics' is demonstrably fiction. Not for the first or last time, Blair rewrites his political biography. In submitting himself to Macmurray, Blair was not in any way being baptised into mere politics; he was being 'saved', preparing to enter the Kingdom.

For Macmurray had become a great one on Despair, a word he would place in his books in italics; and, of course, he was therefore addressing himself to the very condition suffered by young Tony. My gurus, when I was young, taught me the wise adage: 'Beware when you find what you are looking for.' Tony Blair could have done with that advice, although it is improbable that he would have found it acceptable, for the lure of a philosopher who claimed that he not only knew the source of despair but also an unfailing antidote was, for Blair, irresistible. Needless to say, such extravagant claims could not be made in the context of politics but only in religious terms; and the ultimate resolution that Macmurray taught was that proposed by hundreds of vicars throughout Britain every Sunday morning – celebration of the fellowship of all things in God.

Macmurray's reputation as a philosopher deservedly did not survive the war and before his death he had been relegated to a minor figure in academic theology; but with the potential prime minister of Britain persisting in telling us in 1994: 'If you really want to understand what I'm all about, you have to take a look at a guy called John Macmurray. It's all there', some scrutiny of Macmurray's dated mixture of homespun psychology and on the hoof sociology has to be endured. Not 'all is there', but it does become clear why of all the masks Blair wears to deny and conceal his wounds, Macmurray is the one he finds most comfortable.

What Blair has plundered from Macmurray comes from the moralist's distinction between Society and Community. For Macmurray, the term Society refers to 'those forms of human association in which the bond of unity is negative or impersonal'. He illustrates this assessment of Society by proposing that: 'Hobbesian society is based on force, Rousseau's on consent, but both are aimed only at the protection of the individual associates in the pursuit of their private interests.' In contrast, Community associations have 'positive personal relations as their bond ... it is a personal not impersonal unity of persons'. This philosopher, ever the preacher, tells us the path to be taken is away from the negative societal values – they are based on a

> categorical misconception, a misconception of one's own nature which must affect all our actions for we shall misconceive our own reality by appearing to ourselves to be what we are not, or not to be what we are ... It is a misconception that is 'categorical', making action

inherently self-frustrating, for in the end such a misconception leads us only to the discovery that all objectives have the same illusory character; this is the experience of *despair*.

And then, lest his student listeners – who were the bewildered Blairs 20 years before Blair himself read the published lectures – should find the professor taking them out of their depth, he repeats himself in a simple homily:

> When two friends quarrel and are estranged each blames the other for the bad relations between them. Or, to put it otherwise, if my motivation is negative then I appear to myself as an isolated individual who must act for himself and achieve whatever he can by his individual efforts, in a world which cares nothing for success or failure. Yet in reality, my isolation is self-isolation, a withdrawal from relationships through fear of the other. This attitude which expresses the experience of frustration and despair is nothing but the sophisticated adult version of the attitude of the child whose mother refuses to give him what he wants. Its unsophisticated formula is 'nobody loves me'.

It is not surprising that the isolated Blair resonated to such a diagnosis; and no less unsurprising that he responded to the balm Macmurray proceeded to apply to his wounds:

> If we isolate one pair as the unit of personal community we can discover the basic structure of community as such. The relation between them is positively motivated in each. Each then is heterocentric; the centre of interest is in the other not himself. The other is the centre of value. For himself he has no value in himself, but only for the other; consequently he cares for himself only for the sake of the other.

However:

> If their relationship to the other is negative ... this will destroy the realisation of the exclusive relationship itself. To be fully positive, therefore, the relation ... must be inclusive and without limits. Only so can it be a community of persons. The self-realisation of any individual person is only fully achieved if he is positively motivated towards every other person with whom he is in relation.
>
> We can therefore formulate the inherent ideal of the personal. It is a universal community of persons in which each cares for all the others and no one for himself ... if the negative motive could finally and completely be subordinated to the positive, in all personal activity, the redemptive function of religion would be complete; and only its central activity would remain. Religion would then be simply the celebration of community – of the fellowship of all things in God.

Macmurray's instruction brought Blair to the Lord, but not to the Labour Party. No one could have been more anti-political than Macmurray, and if he had the stamina to hack through the thicket of Macmurray's often dense prose, the only serious politics he would have discovered was Macmurray's tirade against Marx's irreligious doctrines. Macmurray, as a young man, had translated some of the early Marx but his early flirtations with Marx are vigorously repudiated in the late works to which Blair had access and which so moved him. In seeking to persuade his biographers that he found his brand of socialism via Macmurray in Oxford, he is proffering credentials which he does not possess. I have no taste for politicians offering false political prospectuses, or for those who, to gain credibility, would adapt their own CVs according to the circumstances of the time.

If it were not for Blair's repeated and misleading assertions that Macmurray is the source from which his membership of the Labour Party sprang, one would pay scant attention to his undergraduate infatuation with philosophy and religion. A young man going through a delayed adolescence, assailed by new and, to him, frightening awakenings, turning to religion, is a commonplace phenomenon, oft remarked upon, not least by Byron:

> In thoughts like these true wisdom may discern
> 　Longings sublime, and aspirations high,
> Which some are born with, but for the most part learn
> 　To plague themselves withal, they know not why:
>
> 'Twas strange that one so young should thus concern
> 　His brain about the action of the sky;
> If *you* think 'twas philosophy that this did,
> 　I can't help thinking puberty assisted.

Young Blair, in his philosophical meanderings, was provided by Macmurray with a religious base that could support him in his personal travail; but the self-abnegation which Macmurray urged upon his acolytes was clearly unacceptable to Blair's exhibitionism, so he took Macmurray à la carte and later, after Oxford, chose another vehicle, the Labour Party, which he hoped could carry him away, would distance himself from his own Furies. But meantime in Oxford, buoyed up by Macmurray, he faced the world with that now well-known toothy smile, the butt of so many caricatures, with a countenance that persuaded the president of St John's, Sir Richard Southern, to remark in his end-of-term report in 1974: 'Seems extraordinarily happy'. Extraordinarily is the apposite word; maniacal evangelical persuaders rarely totally convince the sophisticated. The president seems sceptical, and evidently was on enquiry, asserting in his final 1975 report: 'Needs to be tougher in thinking through his ideas', a criticism which, 20 years later, causes us to admire the president's perspicacity.

When Blair eventually arrived in the Labour Party he came garbed in vestments stolen from Macmurray's wardrobe; he had selected his plunder with care, rejecting the ill-fitting, those that mortified his address, and choosing only those that he found were custom-made for his figure. Repeatedly, during his short political life, these are the clothes he wears.

The moral philosopher taught friendship, pure unadulterated friendship, free from 'negative' motivation, as the basic structure of the ideal community. He spelled out to the priest who had taken Blair to Macmurray 'that the noblest form of human existence is friendship'; that in friendship, as in community, antagonism and estrangement lead only to 'despair'. This immature Boy Scout ethos pervades Blair's political thinking; never a speech goes by without him calling for 'partnership'. The model of the altruistic 'friendship', the 'pair', which is the starting-point of Macmurray's discovery of his 'universal community', is a fable which may beguile those moved by tales of chivalry, even as Blair's tales of partnership between Government and Industry, between the Labour Party and the City, between Capital and Labour, although leached away from reality, attract all those seeking an illusory safe political option.

The essential congruence between the mode of thought of Macmurray and his disciple is their neurotic denial of the simultaneous existence of contradictory feelings or attitudes which envelop every human relationship and which is endemic to all born of woman. Both these men seek to disavow ambivalence; they cannot tolerate, and hence cannot acknowledge, the coexistence of love and hate.

When Macmurray selected as his model for the 'community' the 'pair', the pair he chose was 'friendship', not flesh and blood lovers, for passion, with all the tumult that must bring, overtly shows what Macmurray seeks to mask: the opposite to love is apathy, not hate, and throughout our lives the ambivalence we have towards our first carer, wanting full, absolute and unconditional love and simultaneously resenting our dependence, is a concomitant, as every school of depths psychology affirms, of all our later relationships. Afraid of his own resentment, fearful that aggressiveness against the 'other' may lead to the destruction of the carer upon whom he depends,

Macmurray stumbles upon basic Freudian insights as he warns against what he describes as 'negative' feelings; and significantly, to explicate his philosophy, he admonishes us to repudiate those feelings, for they bring us despair, the frustration 'of the child whose mother refuses to give him what he wants'.

Macmurray correctly diagnoses the source of our discontent but his proposed remedy, the banishment of all aggression, may be an option open to saints on their way to heaven but it is unavailable on this earth. Meantime, for some afflicted with 'negative' feelings so murderous that they are ever fearful of the consequences of releasing any aggression, religion may be of assistance; in Macmurray's case, predictably, his renunciation of aggression led him to the supreme practitioners of absolute pacifism, and before his death he had joined the Quakers. The same syndrome embedded in Blair's consensus politics prompts him to attempt to de-politicise the Labour Party and proffer policies expressing his love to all and his hostility to none, excepting only those who would dare to disturb his conflict-free dreams; any voice heard to say the emperor has no clothes is, in Blair's infelicitous phrase, 'in need of therapy'. By the autumn of 1995, while he basked in the warm approbation of the tabloid *Sun*, his displeasure that his consensus politics should even be queried led him to accuse the *New Statesman*, *Guardian* and *Tribune* of producing 'claptrap written as fact'.

To unravel this curious convoluted but fanatical insistence of Blair's upon consensus by diktat, we need to take the unguarded hint of his mentor, who warned that 'negative' feelings, breaking up consensual relations, would bring about the despair 'of the child whose mother refuses to give him what he wants'. Unwittingly, Macmurray points us to seek elucidation of his and Blair's shared idiom of thought not from philosophers or politicians but from the paediatrician; and we are encouraged in such an exercise by a no less unguarded hint of Blair's when, replying to an interviewer wanting to know what had brought him into politics, he gave the distinctly odd and evasive reply: 'Well, I suppose you could go into all the slightly twee motives.'

'Twee', sweet, dainty are certainly not words one associates with adult male motivation; it is a colloquialism that belongs to the description of the world of childhood and it is in that world we can find the sources of Blair's fantasy of a politics without discordance or schism.

No one in Britain in this century has more elegantly addressed himself to those sources than the fortunately influential paediatrician Donald Winnicott, and his teachings have resulted in many children receiving the sensitive care which lays the foundation of a confident sense of identity. Those denied such care may, by impersonation, on stage, in politics, or in their daily lives, be forever borrowing someone else's persona; but those blessed with a mother tuned into her baby's emotional needs have the greater opportunity as adults to possess a secure ego. The empathising mother, letting the child feed at his own time, willingly allowing him, within her own embrace, to sleep peacefully and restfully, gives him the most complete experience of security possible in human life; this is where the foundation of identity rests. I am because I *feel* secure and, therefore, real; and since the feeling 'I am' leads to the question 'What am I?' it brings the experience of 'being' and leads on to the growth of self-consciousness, self-knowledge and self-realisation.

But Winnicott, like the psychoanalysts WRD Fairbairn and Harry Guntrip in their seminal works, gives warning of the consequences of those unblest as children with such empathising carers. No one can regain the paradise lost linking us to the cosmos within the womb. As the ancient Jewish saying recounts: 'In the mother's body man knows the universe, in birth he forgets it.' But as far as the initial pre-natal condition can be recaptured, it comes from the mother knowing her babe by feeling and identification. Winnicott has taught us that the motility that exists in the intra-uterine life as the babe kicks in the womb, and that exists when a babe of a few weeks thrashes away with his limbs, is the precursor to the aggression that has to be positively organised by the child if he is to become a person. And for that to successfully come about, the babe, without overwhelming fear, must constantly discover and rediscover the environment by using his motility as he snuggles and struggles within his mother's arms; and thus, and only thus, he can enjoy the primal erotic experience within which he can fuse his love and aggression.

But what of those who, by environmental chance or by less than good enough mothering, have been denied the circumstance which permits such a fusion to take place, those who are not provided with the series of individual experiences which enable them to learn that, despite the aggression they felt against their first provider, despite their hatred of their dependency and their anger that, to adapt Macmurray's phrase, the mother 'refused to give them what they wanted', despite all their 'negative' murderous wishes, they were still secure in their mother's love? One of the variants in adult behaviour which tells of such an early determining pattern, marked by empathetic disharmony, is, I believe, seen in Macmurray's pacifism and Blair's consensus politics. Those unconsciously terrified that their aggression, unglued to love, is so dangerously at large that it would bring dire punishment upon them, make the vain attempt to outlaw it entirely; but aggression, like sex, will out, and if repressed, not faced, governed or constructively sublimated, can bring about similar distortions of the human spirit. It may be that such attempts to banish aggression can, within a religious context, have some benign consequences for the worshipper and society; and it could be urged that in the politics of Gandhi's India they had an honourable place. But in the politics of contemporary Britain, it has one certain consequence: it will end in tears.

Already at the TUC conference of 1995, unlike the Labour Party conference a month later, there were overt intimations of the turbulence lying ahead. Never have I observed Blair so uncomfortable, so uncertain, as he faced the suspicious delegations wary of the man who wishes to distance them from government, and who would deny them the right to pursue aggressively their demand for wage-earners to have a greater share in national income, a share now running at its lowest level since records began in 1955.

The delegates did not need the confirmation of the Central Statistical Office telling us that had wages maintained the same share of GDP as in the mid-1970s, employment income would now be more than £60 billion higher than it is; this translates into a loss, compared with what might have been, of £2,750 a year for every worker. One of the oldest economic debates in which the trade unions have played so prominent a part is about how the national cake is, or should be, divided. That is the battleground on which the struggles between labour and capital have taken and will take place; and, presently, capital is winning hands down. No wonder that the delegates were sullen; and no wonder that some of the leaders immediately after the conference expressed to me in private their contempt for what they regard as Blair's naïvety, his belief that in the social market capitalism would be wooed into voluntarily accepting the need for social justice. Less eloquently, but certainly no less robustly, they put the view expressed by Hugo Young: 'Labour, the tyro party of capitalism, has yet to understand the full brutality of the capitalistic logic.'

Young's appreciation of the lack of understanding in this respect of Blair's Labour is accurate. There may be some 'modernists' within the trade union movement content to convert unions into Friendly Societies, ready to accept that the trade union movement, a creation of the industrial age, will in the long run be a casualty of an information revolution causing future job creation to be in small non-unionised companies and ensuring that an increasingly large chunk of the labour force will be self-employed; but such defeatism is not a dominant view. If Blair's political memories of the Wilson era were less selective, less determined by his temperament, he would, while updating Wilson's 'white heat of technology' presentation, also recall the fall of the Labour government as it vainly attempted to impose a consensus backed by penalties upon the trade unions. Winters of discontent will assuredly follow any *In Place of Strife* attempts that dreamily postulate that industrial peace can be obtained without acknowledging the reality that in a genuine democracy, whatever corporate states may be able to do, works councils or some such employer–employee structures may contribute to industrial harmony but cannot end the inherent antagonism between capital and labour.

It is not only the fat cats of the privatised utilities who make this glaringly obvious; management throughout a capitalist society will look after themselves and, as they conceive it to be their duty, look after their shareholders. On many occasions during my stewardship of my constituency I was called in by unions and, not infrequently, by employers to help prevent or resolve industrial disputes. I learned to distinguish between what was intractable, the antagonism of capital and labour, and what was tractable. What was important was the creation of a balanced truce in which each side knows its clearly defined boundaries, presses them to the limits, but knows that overstepping them leads to disaster for all. The trade unionist who had, in my youth, a considerable political influence upon me was that lovable communist Arthur Horner. During his presidency of the South Wales miners, the coal fields were almost strike-free; his controlled aggression was feared by the owners and he knew how to take his miners to the very edge but not, like the paranoid Scargill, over the edge.

The delegates at the TUC 1995 conference, with the television cameras focused upon them, out of loyalty to the Labour movement, not to Blair, dutifully gave the required standing ovation to the Labour leader; but the delegates had sat on their hands as sceptically and sullenly they listened to his call to have 'a revolution in our attitudes at work, in management, in unions, in government. All of us need to address a new agenda. Instead of conflict, partnership.' Blair felt a cold wind blowing into his cosy kitchen cabinet. It was a wind from a real outside world 'swept with confused alarms of struggle and flight', where ignorant and not so ignorant armies clashed by night and, indeed, by day, a world that cannot be wished away.

The alarm bells were ringing, awakening Blair's personal

aides; if the 1995 Labour Party conference was to be all consensus, sweetness and light, ground had to be yielded. Privately, Blair or his authorised aides held talks with union leaders and accepted that the reduction of the union vote at Labour conferences to 50 per cent was to be the final settlement, and other specific commitments were given. It was to be announced at the conference that a Labour government would put money in union coffers by abolishing the restrictions on check-off and by introducing legislation giving unions the statutory right to recognition if 50 per cent of a workforce balloted for it; the principle of the national minimum wage would be affirmed; compulsory competitive tendering, uncompromisingly opposed by local government unions, would, under Labour, be abolished; railways would be brought back into public ownership; and the commitment to full employment as a goal of policy both domestically and in Europe would be unequivocal.

Old Labour, through the unions, thus obtained a respite; but it was to be a short pause. A government that genuinely fulfils the commitments of the 1995 Labour conference would not find in place an approving national consensus; there would be fierce resistance in many quarters. So in 1996, true to the weaknesses of his temperament, Blair came up with his Big Idea: the Stakeholder Society, where the lion would lie down with the lamb, and all would be peace; each man and woman possessing the sense of belonging in workplace and boardroom; trust restored between stakeholder-worker and business; unemployment tackled at its source; abdication of power by corporation and unions and interest groups – all combining to empower the individual, all holding hands in one great happy John Lewis Partnership. Apple pie and motherhood and Amen.

Only a few spoilsports could doubt such a vision; most enthusiastically rummaged through the runes of the brave declarations, and there found their salvation. But a few asked the needed foreboding questions. Anatole Kaletsky, the economics editor of *The Times*, doubted whether Blair would ever move from the hideous business school jargon of the stakeholding society to the language of social revolution; to tackle unemployment at source would require a transformation in the conduct of economic policy in Britain. The minimum would be root and branch reform of the Treasury and the Bank of England, including the removal of most of their senior officials, and a total repudiation of the monetarist orthodoxy that government must never take risks with inflation sternly endorsed by Blair.

And the *Independent on Sunday* reported the not dissimilar dismayed response of Peter Townsend:

'I have been on Labour policy committees for 30 years,' said Professor Peter Townsend, the country's leading authority on the welfare state, 'and I'm despondent ...' Professor Townsend said that all the talk about giving the unemployed a stake would be meaningless unless Labour was prepared to change its cautious economic policies and commit itself to creating jobs in the public sector and fostering new industries. 'You can't train people for jobs that aren't there,' he said, and then he highlighted the great problem hidden by Blair's One Nation rhetoric.

What happens when stakes (or, to be very Old Labour, classes) conflict?

Traumatic Families

Sociologists have paid much attention to what they describe as 'homogamy'. Homogamy means that people are attracted to one another because they are similar in character, family and social background, and experiences. This unexceptional and prosaic observation has, however, more recently been considerably sophisticated as the sociologists, confirmed by the clinical findings of psychotherapists and reinforced by the clinical findings of the paediatrician John Bowlby and his followers, have directed greater attention to the phenomenon. Now they stress that the catalyst precipitating attractions may often be hidden, that the less obvious similarities may be more determined and decisive, and that, in particular, those who have undergone separate but similar early traumatic family experiences, resulting in parallel later emotional problems, can be compellingly attracted to one another. The sociologists illuminating the condition claim their research reveals that bonding between those who have endured traumatic childhoods can be so intense that it can come into existence without the protagonists being in any way consciously aware of the dynamic behind their motivation, and indeed sometimes even in the absence of any verbal communication.

The bold sociologist David Aberbach has insightfully put forward the hypothesis that this silent bonding operates beyond the area of personal relations; that there are circumstances when it comes into play between a political leader and the society in which he dwells.

> Much as individuals silently bond with each other on the basis of shared trauma, so also a society and leader may bond together when external crisis intersects with private trauma.

The lives of Tony and Cherie Blair, and the relationship between Tony Blair and the electorate, provide a surfeit of clinical material validating the sociologist's conclusion.

Blair hesitates to recall the full agonies that, during his childhood, enveloped his family. Justifiably he dismisses a suggestion of his critics that because he went through the private educational system, finishing at Oxford, 'it must have been a bed of roses'. 'Don't get me wrong. It was a happy childhood,' he protests and disavows, 'but it did seem as though I was spending every spare minute in Durham hospital visiting … and there was a lot of worry and uncertainty attached to that.' He concedes that the disabling stroke suffered by his father was 'one of the formative events' in his life. But he draws back from commenting on the anguish the 'event' brought him; rather, he emphasises the beneficial instruction it brought: 'My father's illness impressed on me from an early age that life was going to be a struggle, that there were a lot of losers.' That seems as far as he is able to acknowledge the effect on him of the family turmoil.

More usually he attempts to distance himself entirely from the pains he suffered as a child; he strives, as at the 1995 Labour conference, to displace them from the private to the public area, to eloquently but overdeterminedly emphasise the overriding importance of the stable family, and to denounce the iniquities that result from its instability. 'Look at the wreckage of our broken society. See Britain through the eyes of our children. Are we really proud of it? Drugs, violence, youngsters hanging round street corners with nothing to do.'

Families can be destabilised not only by separation; other early traumas endured by children and adolescents also result in the catalogue of vices enumerated by Blair. His catalogue is, however, not exhaustive and if it were more comprehensive, it would also note that whatever the lifelong burden personally carried by the traumatised children and adolescents, society very occasionally can be the beneficiary as well as the victim; and, indeed, sometimes in the person of a political leader with a history of traumatised childhood or adolescence, society can be both beneficiary and victim.

My generation has felt the full force of political leaders who, after being traumatised by severe loss, neglect or upheaval in their early years, established for a while an astonishing rapport with their nation; a homogamous relationship bound them together, a relationship founded on the affection one had for the other because of common strength but, more usually, common frailties. Such leadership is hazardous, sometimes bringing benefits but too often bringing disasters. Hitler's brutalised childhood was within a family that suffered early multiple losses culminating, when he was 14, in the deaths of his father and, a short time later, of his mother. Stalin lost three siblings in early childhood and his father at 11. And Churchill had an appalling childhood; his son, Randolph, conceded: 'The neglect and lack of interest in him shown by his parents were remarkable even by the standards of late-Victorian and Edwardian days.' Leaders emerging traumatised from the epicentre of domestic upheaval and loss need to be especially scrutinised; and Blair is such a leader.

For the doleful consequences of the blows that concussed the Blair family in Tony's childhood are far-reaching; they are not limited to his attempt within a public life to overcome the personal feelings of estrangement which acutely dog him. His was not, as he claims, 'a happy childhood'; it was a terrorised childhood, and the *mésalliance*, substantially involuntary and irrational, between Blair and large sections of the electorate is a bonding between an alienated man and an alienated society, each attempting within an homogamous relationship, to find a magic analgesic to relieve them of their pains, to heal their wounds and erase their scars.

It is true that there can emerge leadership of inspirational character when, at a particular time, a member's agonising private experiences correspond with, and become virtually symbolic of, the group. Weber long ago illustrated unforgettable correspondences of this type. Hosea's marriage to a prostitute symbolises the 'prostitution' of ancient Israel; Jeremiah's childlessness represents national loss and barrenness and brings home the fact that procreation on the eve of mass slaughter and exile by the Babylonians is futile; the death of Ezekiel's wife is a symbol of the destruction of the Temple in Jerusalem, to which the Judaeans were 'wedded' in faith.

These ancient Jewish prophets did not speak in mellifluous tones to their people; they did not collude with them, gloss over their frailties. They identified the evils in their society and raged in memorable language against those who perpetrated them. There was no compromise with iniquities. The New Jerusalem was not to be reached by temporising; they certainly did not believe the route was via the middle ground. Such men, however, are not the exemplars chosen by our contemporary puny politicians. The prophets suffered grievous losses, infertility, infidelity, death of near ones, but they were the exceptional men whose traumas were transmuted into creative leadership; they mastered grief by transforming it into a creative motivation.

For most ordinary mortals, being traumatised by loss or upheaval in their early days results in inescapable chronic handicap. For a few individuals, however, the grief, the residual anger and depression which can spring from their earlier setbacks, the idealisation and alienation which have resulted, contribute to their becoming political leaders. Unfortunately, whatever leadership early trauma yielded in biblical times, the experience of the Western world in the twentieth century tells us that our prophets have all been false prophets. In certain limited circumstances they can be of considerable social and political use, as is witnessed by Churchill in the war years. But the general rule is that when a traumatised leader suddenly emerges as a microcosmic correlative and symbol of a specific and usually transient societal condition, then trouble lies ahead.

In Blair's case, all his dissimulations cannot mask the severity of his early trauma. In an instant all the hapless boy's security was shattered as a massive stroke reduced his towering father to a speechless babe. Financial constraints immediately imposed themselves upon the patriarchal family. Like many men of Leo Blair's background and generation, a working wife would have been regarded as subversive of the husband's authority. This was a widespread view, one I found deeply embedded in the culture of the mining villages of my constituency, where, up to the late 1960s, a miner who let or encouraged his wife to work was despised. So Hazel could not seek outside employment to supplement the now diminished family income. New school uniforms became hand-me-downs, treats became rare, planned foreign holidays abandoned.

There had already been little anchorage in the family as Leo climbed out of his class, living in rented, sometimes austere, accommodation, moving from one town to another, from Edinburgh to Glasgow, even as far as Adelaide in Australia, and then on to Durham, forever seeking to improve on his lowly positions. Geography and the desperate uncertainties of upward mobility had continuously destabilised the family during Tony's short life. A family so utterly dependent upon the father as it moved peripatetically between different environments could, with such a history, have been ill-prepared to receive the shock when the pilot who had literally steered them round the world utterly lost his direction.

In a curious attempt to deny his essential rootlessness Blair, in 1994, was claiming that in Durham he had been influenced as a child by the traditional socialism of the Durham miners, 'a feeling which has stayed with me ever since'. By what process of osmosis this took place is not explained; his childhood was in the shadow of the cathedral at Durham, a city which has a very different feel from the surrounding area, and in any event, by the time Blair came to live in Durham most of the pits in the county had been closed. Blair's romantic recall has little credibility; his creation of an imaginary evocation does tell us of his sense of loss of lineage.

His wandering father had bequeathed him only a Romany inheritance and had deprived him of any tradition of strong religious conviction, of commitment to socialism or firm attachment to class or locality. A few months after his fanciful nostalgic excursion to his Durham childhood, in another interview he truthfully acknowledged: 'We moved around a lot when we were young ... I never felt myself very anchored in a particular setting or class.' And thus, inadequately anchored, young Blair was, by a cruel fateful wind, blown from his frail moorings.

In later life this nomadic childhood contributed to his facility to move with ease from one piece of political territory to another; not all of us have a taste for the gypsy political life, but he is a man untutored in reverence for the fixed place of abode, the new holds promise, the old is discarded. Converting his original handicap into personal political advantage and persuasively claiming it was to national advantage, he has on the political plain succeeded in making lability a virtue and fealty a sclerotic disease.

But the trauma inflicted on the singularly vulnerable ten-year-old, unlike his family vagabondage, does not lend itself to being so artfully used in the public arena. However cunning the handler, it remains too explosive to be displaced from private psyche to public argument, for it is charged with the retaliatory threat of what Ernest Jones, one of the greatest Welshmen of this century, the carrier of psychoanalysis from Vienna to the Anglo-Saxon world, described as aphanisis, the terrible condition of a living death where all sexual desire in any form, however attenuated, is utterly and irrevocably extinguished. It brings a fear even more profound than the fear of castration, and Jones, following Freud, asserts it can arise from the death wish which, in our ambivalences, we unconsciously direct against our loved ones: '... each man kills the thing he loves, By each let this be heard'.

And when the death actually occurs, when our buried death wishes are seemingly fulfilled, attributing omnipotence to our evil thoughts, burdened with guilt, irrationally taking responsibility for the death, we fear awesome retaliation will result, that we will, as murderers, suffer the deserved punishment. Freud tells us:

> A hostile current of feeling ... against a person's nearest and dearest relatives may remain latent during their lifetime, that is, its existence may not be betrayed to consciousness either directly or through some substitute. But when they die this is no longer possible and the conflict becomes acute.

And then, comfortingly, Freud adds that the taboo against acknowledging the retaliatory fears can, through a mourning process, fade away:

> When in the course of time the mourning runs its course, the conflict grows less acute, so that the taboo upon the dead is able to diminish in severity or sink into oblivion.

But what if, as occurred to Blair's father, death strikes but does not slay, leaving the victim dumb but with accusatory eyes staring for years, day in and day out, at his wretched little son, denied the relief of mourning, denied 'the course of time' when 'the mourning runs its course' and 'the conflict grows less acute ... is able to diminish in severity or sink into oblivion'.

With the stricken father lying in the house, young Blair was compelled to live for years with the threatening consequences of

his unconscious ambivalences to his father; and the usual
Oedipal rivalries that are part of all our growing up would
inevitably have been continuously stoked up as his mother was
compelled to give her whole attention to her helpless husband.
When one remarks upon Blair's constant and repeated retreat
from acknowledgement of ambivalence in his public discourse, a
mode of thought which frequently invalidates his political
judgement, here is one of the sources: each resentment felt
against the appurtenances of the illness enveloping the
household would have brought new guilts, renewed fears of
retaliatory action. No wonder that, like his mentor Macmurray,
any sign of ambivalence is interpreted by him as a red light
warning him of dangers ahead.

Young Blair's burdens could not be shared with his siblings.
His older brother was away at public school and, to add to his
woes, even as his mother's attention was still directed to the
slowly recovering father, yet another catastrophe suddenly
engulfed the family. Still's disease, a form of infantile
rheumatoid arthritis which erodes the cartilage and eventually
burns out the joints, hit his youngest sister, who was to spend two
years in hospital as doctors battled to save her life using toxic
immuno-suppressant drugs which had distressing side effects.

The boy therefore entered his teens fearful that he was being
pursued, frightened that he would be the next victim of a hostile
invisible disabler intent on mowing down his family; for Blair
lived in a house of secrets, in a haunted household where ghosts
stalked – the ghosts of the wild promiscuous mother of Leo, the
mother of whom no one dared speak or enquire, and the spectre
of Leo's irresponsible musical father whose names, genuine and
assumed, can never be erased from Anthony Charles Lynton
Blair's birth certificate.

Blair, incredibly, claims that until recently he had no idea of
the origins of his Christian names. He told his biographer, Jon
Sopel, that it came as a bombshell when, midway through his
leadership campaign, the *Daily Mail*, in revealing the truth about
his grandparents, pointed out that Blair's middle names, Charles

Lynton, came from the music-hall grandfather, Charles Parsons, whose stage name was Jimmy Lynton. Blair said he had never questioned why he was given these names; he simply assumed it was a family tradition. And when his older brother was contacted by the prurient press, he corroborated Tony's response. He was nonplussed: 'The names Charles Parsons and Jimmy Lynton don't mean a thing to me.'

That Tony Blair should have raised no questions about having three Christian names is just possible; that he should have not queried his conventional second name is credible; but that he and his brother never queried why he had the curious third Christian name, is surely because they knew that was a question they must never ask. Tony Blair has told his biographer that he 'had known his father had been adopted but it was something Leo did not speak about and equally something the children didn't ask about'. That was secret, forbidden territory.

Even although we may wish to conceal it from ourselves, those of us who are parents know how within a household children will divine the existence of our secrets; and when they know a secret exists, but one to which they have no access, then left in ignorance of its details, the secret can become more not less menacing and the emotional content of the parents' secret, one they feel is too agonising to expose, is passed on. There is, unhappily, these days a grim plenitude of clinical material illustrating how far-reaching the deleterious effects can be of the unarticulated traumas of parents upon their children; the children of the silent scarred survivors of the Holocaust, like the children of the guilty murderous Nazis, can both become victims of the parents who cannot bring themselves to talk of the horrors of their past.

Freud, in his *Totem and Taboo*, long ago spelled out how vain was the attempt by one generation to conceal their traumas from their successors:

> We may safely assume that no generation is able to conceal any of its more important mental processes from its successor. For psychoanalysis has shown that

everyone possesses in his unconscious mental activity an apparatus which enables him to interpret other people's reactions, that is, to undo the distortions which other people have imposed on the expression of their feelings. An unconscious understanding such as this of all the ... dogmas left behind by the original relation to the father ... make it possible for later generations to take over their heritage of emotion.

It is such a 'heritage of emotion', a transgenerational pathology, with which Tony Blair wrestles. At a time when the shame, and the legal disabilities, of illegitimacy were real, his father, after initially as a baby being dragged from lodging-house to lodging-house while his parents were on tour, was soon to be treated as an encumbrance, and was dumped as a little boy on the family of the Glasgow ship-rigger James Blair. Neither of the two biographers of Blair tells us at what age his father was wrenched away from his natural parents, or whether he entered a house where there were other children. Indeed, both biographers display surprisingly little curiosity about Tony Blair's grandparents. Even in John Rentoul's more detached biography, the biographer naïvely and dogmatically asserts 'the story of Tony Blair's real grandparents is a colourful one, although perhaps of limited relevance to all but genetic determinists'. But I believe that traumas endured by Tony Blair's father continue to reverberate.

The actor-politician able to play, in politics as he did on stage, many parts, possessing a political agility which enables him with excessive fluidity to discard the old for the new, reflects the identity confusions which can so often afflict the adopted child unable to model himself upon a certain fixed father figure, ever asking himself what was his sin that caused him to be rejected, uncertain as to who he is, and from whence he came. The essential political rootlessness of Tony Blair, the man who came from nowhere, tells us of the 'heritage of emotion' bequeathed to him by his father.

The burden of such a heritage is not to be minimised. Leo

Blair was one of the thousands of children who, at the time he was placed into what was to be long-term fostering, were treated as the property of parents with children lacking any individual rights and who were able to be disposed of at the caprice of the natural parents. It was the battle that I commenced shortly after I came into the House to erode the discriminatory laws against the illegitimate that brought me to a fuller understanding of the malignant consequences that came from Britain's lack of a comprehensive adoption service giving support and guidance to the unmarried mother as well as to would-be adopters. The unavailability of such a service to all those needing it throughout the country meant that the choosing of new parents by natural parents or by society was little more than a sinister game of roulette with thousands of children often being the losers.

Adoption is an ambitious technical method of resolving sterility, illegitimacy and the nature of the rejected or unattached child; it is also an imaginative and sensitive human enterprise where biology jostles passion, and where irresponsibility, inadequacy or wickedness is met by pity, concern and love. To presume to intervene by laws in this subtle and complex process is to invite condemnation as an intruder; reason and insight embedded within such laws, however mildly corrective, can be speedily resented. Perhaps, in retrospect, it is not surprising that, given the delicacy of the issues, it took me more than a decade to bring about by legislation the needed sweeping changes.

As a solicitor dealing with adoption applications, I had already found, before becoming an MP, that the scores of voluntary adoption societies then in existence were of a strikingly uneven quality. They were unevenly distributed throughout the country, some purportedly serving a locality and others claiming to operate nationally. Many of them had standards of service which were abysmal, lacking professional skills, and dealt only on the basis of bizarre criteria with a selection of adoptive homes and the placement of children with parents who were often considered primarily simply on the basis of their declared religious belief. This dilettante characteristic of so many of the adoption societies was encouraged by the perfunctory surveillance to which, by law, their standards were subject. Indeed, approval of their registration had been reduced to little more than a formality so far as the local authorities were concerned, as they far too often feared to exercise their powers to make their own social work departments act as adoption agencies. Outside the purview of the adoption societies of such varying quality came those adoptions arranged privately by matrons, gynaecologists, solicitors, busybodies or someone a hard-pressed unmarried mother met in the local launderette or fish and chip shop. Choosing parents for someone else's child was in my view certainly too aweful a responsibility to be left to any one person, but the muddlers and the meddlers, who for morbid or mercenary motives were able to intervene to play God, under the laws then in existence were being given a dangerously free hand.

After I had formed an all-party group of MPs committed to pressurising the Home Office to review those adoption and fostering laws, the wind which, following devaluation, blew Jim Callaghan in 1967 out of the Treasury into the Home Office, brought me good fortune in my quest; for both my personal relationship with Callaghan and his own personal biography, which left him with good reason to be concerned with the fate of children unendowed with two ever-present and certain parents, acted in my favour and, despite the department's resistance, he set up, at my request, an advisory committee on which I was to sit. Apart from, for politically correct reasons, one Tory MP being appointed, the other members all already had, as directors of social service departments or adoption societies, as paediatricians, child psychiatrists or jurists, considerable fieldwork experience in adoption. For almost three years we sat taking evidence from all the regions in Britain in our wide-ranging enquiries, and finally produced a unanimous report.

Not waiting for the dust to gather on our recommendations, I persuaded David Owen, then a back-bencher who had drawn in the Private Members' ballot the right to have time to introduce a bill, to sponsor an Adoption Bill. Together we were well advanced in putting through the legislation, when the government, and thus our Bill, fell; the incoming Labour government took over the Bill, which reached the statute book as the Children's Act of 1975. Of all the Acts with which I have been associated, it is the one with which I continue to enjoy an unalloyed satisfaction, for if political life is ever worth the candle, it is when you have persuaded society that it is to be judged by the concern of one generation for the next.

But during the long trawl of evidence-seeking which preceded the Children's Act I learned many lessons and among them, not least, the imperative need to avoid the maladroit placements and concealments of the type which seem to be illustrated by the experience of Leo Blair. He apparently was never formally adopted and his status was left in limbo, enabling his feckless parents, when he was 12, to try to reclaim him. His foster mother evidently attempted to conceal his origins, blotting out his real birthplace in Filey, Yorkshire, and affirming he was born in Glasgow. He was old enough, when his natural parents finally decided to formalise their relationship and his mother married for the third time, to have been likely to have received bewildering intimations that something was afoot; it is clearly possible that at a young age he was aware that he was the child of an adulterous mother, an illegitimacy that would have brought him, in those unenlightened days, a particular shame. That the tensions and ambivalences of his early upbringing pursued him into adulthood is poignantly displayed in his later juggling of his own names and those of his children. When he married, Leo gave his name as 'Blair, formerly Parsons', and took Charles and Lynton, a combination of his natural father's original and stage names, as his middle names. To his first son, William, he gave his foster father's name, James, and Lynton as middle names, and his own middle names, of course, he gave to his second son – although it is evident that he never told them where they came from. The sinister silences that Leo Blair, as a consequence of his early casual and unfeeling placement, imposed upon himself and his family left Tony without the endowment of an authentic father possessing a certain and confident identity. Despite the anchorage provided by the dutiful and stoical mother, the family unit would inevitably have had a fragility ill-equipped to withstand the traumas that fell upon it. The severity of the emotional disturbances resulting from the ambience within which Tony was matured in my view invades both his political and his personal choices; and those who would scoff at such a belief should note the corroboration provided by his significant personal choice.

Wives of politicians, detached from the politics of their husbands, most certainly have as unequivocal a right to privacy as any private citizen. It would indeed be presumptuous to delve into the private life of the diffident Mary Wilson or the politically non-intrusive, kind and eminently sensible Audrey Callaghan, whose warm realism and lack of pretension always left me gratified when I dined with her family at No. 10, as insulated from politics as from the flunkeys and officials below. But that right to privacy can legitimately be denied to wives who actively and enthusiastically join in the political fray. Such a wife is Cherie Blair, who not only shares her husband's considerable abilities but, more relevantly in our quest to uncover the singular relationship between Blair and the electorate, like him she emerges triumphant but scarred from a traumatised family, one in which stagecraft and narcissism had wreaked havoc.

Her actor father, who bears her husband's first name, is the notorious Tony Booth, the 'Scouse git' of the television series *Till Death Us Do Part*. When Cherie was young he abandoned her, her sister, Lyndsey, and her small-time actress mother, Gale. His autobiography, *Stroll On*, makes no reference to his children by Gale except to ask for their forgiveness in the dedication; that request is presumably also directed to the four or five other children he had by other women. He does not even specifically mention Gale in his book. At the time he was supposed to be married to her he presents us with a lewd account of his boisterous 'crumpeteering'. Gale, a tough and brave cookie, meantime gave up the stage and, fortified by a no-nonsense Roman Catholic Labour working-class family background, was prepared for the sake of the children to take on any job – including one in a fish and chip shop. It says much for that woman, as it does for the resource of her daughter, that Cherie is now a highly competent QC.

Given the early adversities endured by Cherie Booth, and the political commitment of her mother's family, it is unsurprising that, unlike her husband, she was already a member of the Labour Party by the time she was 16. She took too from her actress mother an obvious desire to be on stage, and soon put herself forward as the potential Labour candidate to fight Shirley Williams in the Crosby by-election in 1981, the high point of the SDP's march out of the Labour Party; the eyes of the nation were on that by-election and Cherie clearly had an appetite for the publicity such a candidature would attract. Two years later, identifying with the left-wing pressure group the Labour Co-ordinating Committee, she was as candidate for Thanet, speaking on the same platform as Tony Benn, declaring that he had 'inspired' her in her 'quest for socialism' – hardly a claim she would presently make. Opportunism and narcissism would be charges she would require all her considerable forensic skills to ward off today. Indeed some may conclude that, provided she has the opportunity to display those skills publicly, she shows an unseemly readiness to take up causes unbecoming to the wife of a Labour leader; although she may have acted in accordance with the best traditions of the Bar, her championship before an industrial tribunal in October 1995 of a Conservative council against allegations made by some 50 dismissed black and Asian employees alleging racial and sexual discrimination was received with distaste by many in the Labour Party.

But it is in other respects that corroboration which she provides in her partnership with Tony Blair should cause greater public unease. More intelligent than her husband – she gained a

top first in law at the London School of Economics and came top
in the Bar exams, while her husband obtained a second-class
degree at Oxford and an undistinguished third-class at the Bar –
she nevertheless displays disconcerting negative traits, giving
every indication that they flow from her early abandonment and
traumas. Her tenseness and humourlessness, her curious atactic
mien, her much remarked upon public holding of hands with
Blair, her rapturous gazing and kissing of her husband at
conferences, are outward symptoms of much painful insecurity.
At best her early bruising can lead her to champion, for her own
reassurances and those she seeks to aid, causes like Refuge, the
charity that provides accommodation for battered women; and
she speaks out in favour of the Labour document 'Peace at
Home', advocating a national helpline for women victims of
irresponsible violent partners. But less florid and less benign
public consequences can stem from her early bitter experiences.

And those detriments lie in the symmetry that exists in the
family backgrounds of Tony and Cherie Blair, a symmetry that
is a paradigm of the sociologist's developed theory of
homogamy. Both were abandoned by their fathers, the one
literally, the other's powerful father dissolved into dependency;
both act out their lives against theatrical backdrops, the one
bearing the names of the errant actor grandparent illustrating
the Roman adage *nomen omen* – destiny can lie in one's name –
the other burdened by the irresponsible actor father giving her
nothing but a surname; both have responded to dutiful but
insufficiently tender mothering with an obtrusive narcissistic
assertion in their careers; both have used politics and the law to
try and triumph over a parent, while simultaneously fulfilling
the parents' thwarted ambitions, that of being an MP in Leo
Blair's case, and that of being a successful actor in Cherie's case.

The danger of a binding between those who have similarly
disturbed family backgrounds, and undergone similar early
traumas, resulting in comparable emotional problems, is that the
handicaps each partner possesses are compounded, rather than
contained or cancelled out; a *folie à deux* can result. It is true that

there may be many differences between such partners and the attraction may involve a complex matrix of aims and motives; but the homogamic principle is, in the case of the Blairs, too insistently illustrated to permit the symmetry in their personal biographies to be dismissed as coincidence.

At a time when increasingly we have an executive-driven democracy, it is disturbing that we may well have in control in Downing Street a pair who are unlikely, as between themselves, to contain the fall-out from their severe early traumas; on the contrary, it is more probable that the excitations continue or increase as each acts as a mirror to the other. It is a private affair if individuals silently bond with each other on the basis of shared trauma; but a bonding between markedly intelligent and histrionic partners can find a pathological expression in the public domain if their leadership is proffered to a bewildered, insecure society shocked by unmetabolised technological change and frightened by the collapse of traditional and conventional religious values.

An affiliation can arise between such leadership and the estranged afflicted with the fears abounding within a society ridden with anomie. A prosthetic relationship can be established, leader and a fractured electorate each yearning to find in the other a wholeness they lack; but only rarely can such a resolution be accomplished, for this is a bonding infected by pathogenic elements.

Exceptionally, a traumatised leader may for a short period effectively and realistically meet the societal needs. Winston Churchill, forever suffering severe depressions as a result of his traumatised childhood, was such a leader and the historian A J P Taylor emphasised: 'In 1940, any political leader might have tried to rally Britain with brave words, although his heart was full of despair. But only a man who had known and faced despair within himself could carry conviction at such a moment.' But far more usually, as the impossible yearnings of the leader and his followers are increasingly felt to be unfulfilled, disenchantment, often accompanied by disaster, follows. Leaders like

Robespierre, who lost his mother at six and then, together with his siblings, was shortly afterwards totally abandoned by his father; or Ayatollah Khomeini, whose father, when Khomeini was an infant, was murdered by bandits, are far more typical, if somewhat dramatic, examples of traumatised leaders, and tell us of the dire consequences such leadership can bring to a nation.

Within the milder political climate of Britain, with its unwritten constitution of checks and balances, even traumatised dyadic political leadership would not have the capacity to inflict such damage; but the difficulties it could bring should not be underestimated. And in the particular case of the Blairs, one is most certainly not encouraged to believe it is possible, as it was with Churchill, for them to transform their handicap to public advantage, to confront crises and overcome them; for their bonding gives every appearance of being sealed with narcissism.

To bask in widespread public approbation needs an avoidance of expounding discomforting but necessary solutions to public dilemmas. In theory the pain of their traumas could be used to understand, empathise with, confront and resolve the pain within our society, but such a salutary transmutation is unlikely to be achieved by the Blairs. The armourplate of their narcissism acts as a shield against insight. Only if they threw away this defence and were prepared to endure the stress of uncovering the sources of their traumatically conditioned public stances would the electorate be likely to gain advantage from the early sad personal experiences of the Blairs.

The quality of the Blairs' bonding, however, leads one to a pessimistic prognostication, to scepticism that they have the capacity to master the grief of their early years and transform it for the public good into a creative motivation. If one departs from the sociologist's homogamous theory and turns to the schematic distinctions made by classical psychoanalysis when reviewing the motivations operating in one's choice of partners, our pessimism unhappily seems to find increased justification.

Freud, anticipating in 1914 in so many respects the current sociological view, put forward his belief that there are two basic types of choice of a love-object, the anaclitic and the narcissistic. One choice, the anaclitic or attachment option, is governed to a greater or lesser degree by a dependence on images of parental figures. The love-object is selected on the model of parent figures who had guaranteed them, as children, nourishment, care and protection. But the narcissistic choice of partner operates on the model of his relationship to his own self, with the love-object representing some aspect of himself. Freud makes clear that the two types of object choice are to be looked upon as purely an ideal or image, and as liable to alternate or to be combined in any particular case. His exploratory elaborations, however, of the notion of narcissistic choice indicate, in some circumstances, how dominant an element narcissism can become.

Freud set forward a schema for such narcissistic expressions under four headings: a person may love what he himself is, what he himself was, what he himself would like to be and someone who was once part of himself. When Freud writes of the search for a partner who was once part of himself, he has in mind a mother's narcissistic love of her child who was 'once part of herself '. The yearning for someone who was once part of yourself is for someone not necessarily resembling yourself as a unified individual but is rather a wish for someone in whom he can recover and restore his lost unity.

In many cases, of course, some or all of these fourfold elements play a part in our choice of partner that may cumulatively amount to little more than a sharing of a few common traits; but the relationship of the Blairs is not of that order. Their personal biographies, their early traumatic experiences and mothering, have conspired to create an intensely narcissistic bonding. When Cherie avidly publicly gazes at Blair, we recall Narcissus seated by the limpid spring, so fascinated by the sight of his own image that not for a second could he avert his eyes; and so he died of languor.

The myth contains warnings. When a dyadic narcissistic leadership emerges, there can arise a conjunction that is not limited to the immediate protagonists; the psychological traits of the leadership in some circumstances and at some particular times can mirror the general characteristics of society. The private correspondence of the pair extends wider. The 'Me' society, where individualism has been sanctified by Thatcher and her ilk, is singularly vulnerable to the fatal attraction of a leadership that reassuringly confirms, not seriously challenges, its own narcissism; and when, simultaneously, such a leadership proffers a vague communitarianism that, without pain, will relieve the man and woman living in our atomised society, deadened by all the insecurities of menacing and threatening technological changes, then the temptation for electorate and leader, each in a self-induced trance, to consummate the relationship becomes almost irresistible. But such a story would not end in them living happily ever after; there are no never-never lands except in fairy tales.

I have lived through times when political leadership had the courage to call for adult not indulgent infantile responses, when Churchill offered blood, sweat and tears, and when Stafford Cripps, Labour's Chancellor of the Exchequer in the immediate post-war years, successfully called upon the nation to continue its sacrifices, to practise austerity and sharing, so that the foundations could be laid for a fairer society. Can we hope for leadership of this calibre from the Blairs, or will those early traumatic experiences that have so shaped them become, through a symbolic resonance, catastrophically enmeshed in the public domain?

Fellow-Feeling of the Unsound

During and after the 1992 US presidential elections Blair and his young political pups became intemperate disciples of Clinton and his advisers. Dazzled by Clinton's electoral success and interpreting the victory as a triumph for the tactic of abandoning traditional interest groups, rust belts and rainbow coalitions, and appealing to middle suburban America, Blair, despite vigorous protests by John Prescott and 'Old' Labour, imported a copycat campaign and proceeded to Clintonise the Labour Party. 'New' Labour was to follow in the wake of 'New' Democrats.

By 1994 the Clinton programme was in complete disarray; a disenchanted electorate, viewing the shambles, returned a hard-right Republican Congress which proceeded to dismantle all the social and welfare gains made by liberal America over the last generation. Clinton's domestic débâcle has been total; now, often to Europe's danger, he seeks American triumphalism in foreign politics in a desperate and probably successful endeavour to regain popularity. Blair, however, seeing his admired mentor's dissolution, is nonplussed. His biographer John Rentoul concedes: 'Blair's response to Clinton's failure was weak and unconvincing.' Blair, says Rentoul, 'implied that the President lacked the determination to pursue New Democrat policies in office'; 'you don't run on one basis and govern on another'.

But Blair does not dare diagnose the inhibitor which has crippled Clinton's 'determination'; that would bring him to too near an insight into his own dilemma. Blair and Clinton have indeed much in common; it is not, however, simply – as one Tory back-bencher has tartly commented – that 'Blair is Clinton with his zips done up'. What they share and what is so determinant in their conduct of public affairs are the unmetabolised early traumatic experiences which both endured and with which neither has successfully come to terms.

In Clinton, Blair has found a fellow-sufferer, a carrier of the virus which cannot tolerate a seriously conflictual political environment, for that evokes the agonising pains of unendurable early years. The irony, of course, of those politicians afflicted with the virus is that they provoke the very conditions which they desperately wish to avoid. So often unconsciously they recapitulate on the political scene the endless conflicts of their early childhood; and then, having raised the storm, cannot face the tumult.

Clinton never escapes in his politics from this compulsion to re-enact the searing and violent domestic quarrels between his alcoholic stepfather and his self-willed and hot-tempered mother. He has become the centre of controversy in every office he has held. And yet he continues to feel that he must be, as he has said in his own words, 'conflict adverse'. He is entrapped; out of conscious control, he is destined to create turbulences which he then fears to withstand.

To the odd exemplars within his pantheon, from Macmurray to Jagger, Blair, moved by his penchant for narcissistic choices, readily added Clinton, the man whose appalling childhood has so maimed his decisiveness; in Clinton, Blair has found a man whose early traumas exceed even his own. Clinton's father died before the son was born; and the third man the mother then married was a violent alcoholic, ready to display and use a gun in the domestic brawls which were part of the sado-masochistic background to Bill Clinton's childhood. By the time Clinton was 14 years old, the growing son, to protect his mother, was breaking down locked doors to gain entry into rooms where the stepfather was beating up his wife; at 15, Bill Clinton was swearing a deposition against his stepfather after calling the police to the home to arrest the violent man; but the mother, within three months of divorcing him, remarried him. Clinton was fated to be brought up in a household in almost constant disarray, where a minor disagreement could speedily explode into violence.

And that recall dogs him in all his political dealings. An immature electorate, thirsting for 'strong' leadership, within a year of his election had turned on him as awareness grew that rather than confront, rather than face down the vested interests assailing him, Clinton would concede. His self-acknowledged 'conflict adverse' temperament leaves him fair game for his challengers; it was precisely because of what they perceived as his wimpishness that the Republicans, overreaching them-selves, challenged him in 1996 over the US budget deficit issue. Their divisions, and the tactics of Clinton's advisers, temporarily disadvantaged them, but in the end the substantive issues were decided as the Republicans demanded. New Democrats, after all the brave words uttered during the presidential election, have handed over the reins to atavistic America.

Former President Bush once advised us to read his lips; but perhaps in the case of men with the personal biographies of Blair and Clinton, it is not their lips we should read but their persistent smile. Both are nervous smilers, the smiles of men with an almost pathological fear of offending, hiding the anger behind their smiles, fearful of venting their rage. The frequent inappropriateness of their responses found in their countenances is what we can expect from them when they are faced with the political choice fight or flight; always fearful of triggering off the destructive power of their early traumas, too often their response is excessively placatory, desperate to create a consensus when it cannot, or should not, exist. There are lessons to be learned from the fiasco of Clintonism and they are not the ones brought back by Blair's spin doctors. The most important lesson to be learned is a simple one. Beware of smiling politicians.

Rock

At Oxford two passions governed Blair: indifferent to politics and scholarship, his enthusiasms were reserved for religion and rock. Both he pursued with extraordinary zeal. And even as Blair's heavy flirtations with Macmurray's religiosity illuminates his present-day political stances, so does his undergraduate infatuation with Mick Jagger's rock.

His commitment to rock music has proved to be no mere phase-appropriate scream; his was not the transitory allegiance of so many public school boys at Oxford who, released from the artificial constraints of their schooling, in their delayed adolescence, found risk-free liberation in the exuberance of the beat. With Blair his fidelity continues into his 40s. 'Rock music is the absolute love of my life,' he declared in 1995, although characteristically, while declaring for rock in general he refused to specify to his *News of the World* interrogator which were his favourite groups. All for pleasing everyone, when pressed, his response was electorally impeccable: 'All the bands that everybody loves.'

But at Oxford he was less coy about his favourite icon, Mick Jagger. There Blair, as the lead singer in a public school rebel band named The Ugly Rumours, was famed for his Jagger impersonations. His long hair down his back, his purple loons and his cut-off shirt undone to his navel, finger-wagging and punching the air, the man likely to be prime minister of the United Kingdom snarled out his and Jagger's favourite 'Live with Me'. The ambivalences within the well-known words, calculated more to repel than to capture an adult lover, and enveloped in the imagery of the archetypical pre-pubescent nasty little boy, were accompanied by a display of sensuous gyrations, all designed to emphasise the essential androgyny of the singer.

When we see Blair posing in the tabloids with his Fender Stratocaster guitar, throwing a few tentative shapes on the fret board, he demonstrates that he has not forsaken what he has intimated were those 'lazy crazy days' when he 'modestly fronted a college rock group'. His attachment to rock is his present, as well as his past. He recalls his fascination for the Rolling Stones and the Kinks when he so readily presents current magazine music awards, but his presence on such occasions is to him no mere photo-opportunity.

In no sense too is it an exercise in nostalgia, the memory of the early 40-year-old for his early 20s. If it were, it would be readily understood by those of my generation, for when Vera Lynn presided over the 1995 commemorations of VE-Day, for most of us veterans it was her songs above all else that evoked for us our wartime youth, the partings, pains, tragedies and hopes of so formative a period in our lives.

Following upon the publication of my book *Wotan, My Enemy*, which addressed the question of whether it was now possible within the European Union to live with the Germans, I was invited to lecture upon a D-Day cruise of American and British veterans, which ended by accompanying the Queen's yacht as it came up the English Channel. Vera Lynn came aboard our ship; my meeting with her gave me, as it would most ex-servicemen, an extravagant pleasure; and when she sang for us the songs that I had first heard again and again over the tannoy of the troopships sailing in hazardous convoy, the bittersweet emotions they stirred were totally disproportionate to the slightness of the lyrics, simple and banal as they may appear to the more detached.

But the quiddity of those songs, in striking contrast to those coming from the rock icons, is their unequivocal commitment. As wartime youngsters in our 20s we joined with Vera Lynn in a celebration of fidelity; we responded in 'Yours' to a pledge to be joined to our absent lovers until the end of life's story. When, upon our return from distant lands there would be bluebirds again above the White Cliffs of Dover, when the Lights would go on again, it was to be a homecoming to a romantic, tranquil domesticity. There would be the sound of wedding-bells; we wanted to be, or return to be, husbands. We were being hurled across continents from one theatre of war to another, but we were involuntary rolling stones; we wanted to gather moss. We did not believe like Jagger, still revelling in his 52nd year in his inability to find 'satisfaction', that, as he was telling us in his interviews in 1995, the trick in life is to keep on the move.

And there was no misogyny or ambivalence, as in rock music, in our singing; we did not fear entrapment. We wanted to run to our woman, not away from her. 'The archetypical rocker/ rapper,' the *Guardian*'s perceptive Suzanne Moore has observed, 'who regards woman as the "architect of conventional life" is still in revolt, still on the run from mother.' For youngsters rock may be an imaginative space in which they strive to gain their own individuation, to cut the umbilical cord, to find a sexual identity or stretch and indeed escape its limits altogether; the androgynous dimension of their rock idols helps them unthreateningly to engage in what Moore has called 'gender tourism'. Rock can no doubt be such a rite of passage on the way to adulthood and, within its ambit, the bewildered adolescent may temporarily find his bearings; but it is not a place to tarry.

It is because there is a widespread understanding that rock is essentially age-appropriate only that there was so much raillery against the 40- and 50-year-olds who attended the Rolling Stones' 1995 European tour concerts. The comments made at the time by Mark Simpson in the *Independent* were singularly apposite:

> ... pop music must bear a great deal of the responsibility for spreading Peter Pan-itis. Beginning by worshipping youth and turning it into the commodity of the late twentieth century, it has ended up by populating the charts with ghastly mummified spectres like Mick Jagger and Cliff Richard, performers who became stars when they were young but now employ all the technology that royalties can buy to slow the maturation process.

The *Financial Times*'s contributor similarly jeered: 'The 50-something Rolling Stones and their gaga middle-aged fans should accept that youth is gone'; and he approved of the mockery of the kids for the wrinklies, 'because they know that those pumped-up songs and sad pelvic thrusts hide the fact that youth, whether gilded or wasted, is ultimateiy lost'. These 'grown men should have been doing a bit of gardening, polishing their Volvos or topping up their pension plans instead of checking in their adult years at the Wembley box office'. Resentment of this order against the would-be Peter Pans reveals more than vexation with unbecoming juvenilia. It tells us of the subliminal fears that rock encapsulates: the threat that this gender-free music could be emasculating; that this music lures the listener away from his achieved heterosexuality back to the hesitations and diffidences of an androgynous condition with no commitment to another, no responsibilities to flesh and blood women, for in rock's perception women represent everything that the rocker is not: domesticity and social norms. Ambivalence, therefore, towards the adult feminine domain is the defining mark of classic instances of rock rebellion from The Stones to The Doors, Led Zeppelin, The Stooges, The Sex Pistols, Guns N' Roses and Nirvana.

And the current BritPop groups like Oasis and Blur are expressing the same fears of the commitments of adulthood. 'Peter Pan-itis,' Simpson writes:

> seems to have had a peculiar effect on British pop and a new batch of young(ish) acts. The only way to get attention in British pop these days, apparently, is to be derivative and deferential to your ancestors. Bands like Blur and Oasis sound like *Q* readers singing karaoke. Paradoxically, in a world where boyishness is now preferred to manliness everywhere, BritPop seems to have decided that the best way to avoid becoming your dad these days is to impersonate his heroes.

These rock rebels certainly have no wish to become real caring Dads; they are always in retreat from adult mature life. Their defiances should not mislead us into believing that they are brave revolutionaries breaking new ground. Their stance is that of insubordination not that of radicalism. And, in political terms, they are highly suspect for they are secretly complicit with the order against which they affect to revolt. As the music critics Simon Reynolds and Joy Press in their extraordinary, illuminating 1995 work *The Sex Revolt* stress, Jean-Paul Sartre's distinction between the rebel and the revolutionary is apposite when applied to the rocker. For Sartre the rebel's goal is not to create a new and better system; he wants only to break the rules. In contrast, the revolutionary is constructive, aims to replace an unfair system with a new, better system, and is therefore self-disciplined and self-sacrificing. Because of his irresponsibility, the rebel has access to the ecstasy of dissipation and living in the now; the revolutionary, however, enjoys the satisfaction of merging his identity with the collective and long-term projection of improvement whose fufilment lies in the future. 'We take it as read,' write Reynolds and Press, 'that rock is not a revolutionary art, that its insubordination and ego tantrums are complicit with or bound within the terms of capitalism and patriarchy.'

No comfort, therefore, can be obtained from Blair's enthusiasm for rock, no intimations can be obtained there of someone genuinely prepared to challenge and transform the body politic. What can perhaps be deduced from his addiction is his fear of the ebb-tide within rock, dragging the stricken back to androgynous irresponsibility. His overdetermined efforts to resist that dangerous tug lead him, strenuously and tactlessly, and to the offence of many one-parent families, to sing paeans of praise for the traditional family, even as he revels in the music which subverts all its best values. But the reassuring outward respectability of the wide-eyed, fresh-faced, goody-goody, the rock enthusiast who at Oxford, when all around him in his rock circle were taking drugs, listened, he says, to his father's warnings to eschew them, has a widespread appeal to the middle-aged of Middle England. They will not dare to overtly reveal their immaturity by attending today's Rolling Stones concerts but in the secrecy of the ballot-box or in the anonymity of the opinion polls, resonating to the 'freedom' androgyny spuriously offers, they can imagine themselves liberated from their burdens of mortgage and family.

Not all thus respond. The more emotionally adult, sensing the androgyny, find the quality turns them off, not on. Michael Heseltine, in the Commons in 1995, quoted the poem 'A Political Kiss' by Fleur Adcock, who had in fantasy dreamt of kissing John Prescott. That was a rhyme from a woman to a man; but Heseltine would have been more effectively politically mischievous if he had been able to draw attention to another discerning rhyme of Fleur Adcock's:

> Can it be that I was unfair
> to Tony Blair?

His teeth, after all, are beyond compare;
but does he take too much care
over his hair?

If he were to ask me out for a meal,
how would I feel?
Would I grovel and kneel,
aflame with atavistic socialist zeal?
No, I'm sorry, he doesn't appeal:
he's not quite real.

In the House he sounds sincere,
but over a candlelit table, I fear,
his accents wouldn't ring sweetly in my ear.
Oh dear.

I'd love to see him in No. 10,
but he doesn't match my taste in men.

Although rock icons may masquerade as political leaders, grown-up women are wary of their attractions; and, of course, that wariness is reciprocated by the icon. What he wants is not a woman but a sheltering womb. For him, having a real woman brings the threat of parenthood, the quenching of his restless desires and the resolution of his emotional tumult. Rock is enveloped in such fears; and the rock icon's apotheosis by the young and immature comes from such shared apprehensions, anxieties often declared explicitly as, for example, by the group Nirvana.

Nirvana's 1992 multi-million-selling *Nevermind* contains songs like 'Breed' and 'In Bloom' that are riddled with this fear of reproduction and what is perceived as emotional stagnation. Nirvana's work, like so much rock, tells us of what Reynolds and Press have described as 'the regressive impulse to repudiate manhood and seek refuge in the womb'. These music critics draw our attention to the cover of *Nevermind*, which features a baby swimming under water; in front of him dangles a dollar bill on a fish-hook luring him to abandon his amniotic paradise for a corrupt world. Indeed, Nirvana's 1993 follow-up was unequivocally and simply entitled *In Utero*; in its first single, 'Heart-shaped Box', Kurt Cobain, the group's lead singer, begs to be hoisted back to safety with his head in an 'umbilical noose' and declares his longing to be sucked into 'your magnet tar-pit'. He is expressing what so often can be heard amidst rock's clamour: the call to refuse manhood in a world where, the rocker screams, most manifestations of manhood are loathsome. In Cobain's case, his desire to retreat from the world into numbed-out sensuality passed through heroin addiction, then blossomed into a full-blown death-wish, and so he reached his Nirvana; in April 1994 he shot himself. Rock is not always fun; it can be very, very sick. Only the naïve can regard a political leader's infatuation with rock as simply an engaging caprice; it can be as sinister as Hitler's love of Wagner.

For almost invariably the music is in retreat, back to the womb and back to the imagined bliss of the pre-natal condition, back to Mamma, away from reality. Not only Nirvana proclaims its fantasy goal. Dozens of rock music groups assume names telling of their yearnings. Genesis, The New Birth, Babes in Toyland and so many others produce songs or albums confirming the group's longings. Like *In Utero*, *Mothership Connection*, *Mother's Milk*, *Sowing the Seeds of Love*, they are all replete with womb and birth imagery. Indeed, in an arresting 1994 paper, the American Professor of English Alvin Lawson, spelling out the conclusions he draws from his study of rock videos, proposes that the worldwide appeal of much of rock's thumping beat originates in unconscious pre-natal memories of the maternal heartbeat.

Lawson can certainly pray in aid the musicologist to justify his contention, for rock's music rhythm is less simple than it seems.

The tempo of much rock at first appears to be a rapid 100–160 beats per minute or more ... but these false tempos are deceptive because rock drummers usually emphasise alternate beats (often counts 2 and 4 or what in effect are the upbeats), so that the perceived thumping pulse is slower by half. Thus most rock tempos effectively fall into the 60–80 bpm range, about the same as the human heart at rest.

Expressing the view that the rhythmic model of so much rock music is a heart-pulse, Alvin Lawson affirms:

Many bands devise (consciously or otherwise) ingenious rhythmic echoes of the heartbeat sound – for example, three or four quick beats followed by a pause (often played on higher pitch drums, but also by unison guitars or keyboards). The effect simulates an actual pulsing heart. These various heart-pulse rhythmic patterns not only support ... birth/rock music co-relations ... but they also imply that the sonic honorary presence of the maternal heartbeat is more significant than its bpms. Remember that foetal ears are a mere four–six inches from the booming maternal rock beat for most of their first nine months of life – all but a few hours of which pulse along 60–80 times a minute.

It is, however, not only the titles of rock albums or the insistence of the rock beat that are so richly suggestive of the pre-natal and birth events. Rock's central instrumental symbol is Blair's favourite, the guitar; and the guitar's neck which he and fellow-guitarists hold is not only a hesitant phallic intimation; it is also essentially umbilical and, because of its abdominal position and the typically frenzied musician's alternately loving and destructive interactions with it, the guitar's soundbox or body can be seen, and has been so described by Lawson and others, as a placenta.

Such a perception certainly accords with the challenging

conclusions of the psycho-historian Lloyd Demause, who, in order to advance his view of the importance of the psychological imprinting that he contends takes place in foetal life, has assembled an intimidating collection of obstetrical and clinical evidence relating to the rôle of the placenta. It would seem that, during the second trimester, while the amniotic sac is rather roomy, the foetus is able to float peacefully, kick rigorously, turn somersaults, urinate, suck its fingers and toes, grab its umbilicus, become excited by sudden noise, calm down when the mother talks quietly and rock back to sleep as she walks about; but a change of scene in the foetal drama comes about during the third trimester when, as its length and weight increase, the foetus becomes distressed. The crucial problem of the foetus in this newly cramped womb lies in its outgrowing the ability of its placenta to feed it, provide it with oxygen and clean its blood of carbon dioxide and waste. Demause postulates that when the blood coming to the foetus from the placenta is bright red and full of nutrients and oxygen, the foetus feels good, but when the blood becomes dark and polluted with carbon dioxide and waste, the foetus feels bad; the foetus contends, therefore, with a placenta both nutritious and poisonous, alternately or simultaneously.

On such an interpretation the love-hate relationship between rock artists and the placenta-guitar has its precursor in the ambivalence of the foetus to its own placenta; and when the 1960s rock star Jimi Hendrix used to smash and burn his guitar on stage, his violence can be seen as an acting out of the anger of the foetus against the overworked placenta which during birth deprives it of fresh, oxygenated, waste-free blood. Such a display of rage is not peculiar to Hendrix. Many rockers, as in Toad the Wet Sprocket's *Walk on the Ocean* and in Pearl Jam's 1993 show, continue to destroy their guitars. The phenomenon may be an outcrop of mnemonic accumulations originally stored pre-natally as Lawson and Demause appear to suggest; or it may be the product of an extraordinary regressive imaginative fantasy of the rocker. What is unequivocally clear is that it is yet another illustration of the pre-natal and birth imagery which envelops rock, illustrations that are sometimes embarrassingly obvious.

Rock artists clinging desperately, and, in these days of modern sensitive microphones, so unnecessarily, to their microphones and cords, move around like the foetuses that have been photographed clinging to the umbilicus where they find comfort and, it seems, emotional security; and some rock artists, as in Peter Gabriel's video album *P.O.V.*, not content with the subliminal message they are transmitting, have a wrestling match with the mike cord-umbilicus after which they collapse on stage in a foetal position. And often in many rock concerts there is a 'mosh pit', a standing-room-only area at the front of the stage, where in a symbolic birthing ceremony some of the young head-bangers lose consciousness in the crush and are lifted up and 'delivered' to safety on the hands of the crowd. The performing stars often participate in this midwifery rock and at climactic moments in their performances leap, often from risky heights, into the pit, where they are caught and 'delivered'.

Such antics reveal that what the rock star offers is not simply a route to a paradisaical womb insulated from travail – although sometimes this fantasy is on offer – but, rather, he is holding out the opportunity to be reborn. This offer of rebirth is often remarkably explicit. The language of an authoritative musical review of the 1993 performance of the group Smashing Pumpkins of 'Cherub Rock' is so redolent of birth experience, and the nature of audience participation which marked the rendering of the song, enable Lawson to comment confidently:

> Actually, the audience is in deep group perinatal fantasy; entranced by the (remembered maternal heartbeat) rhythm, it identifies (ie, bonds) with the foetus singers/(birth) passion, repeating hypnotically its cry for freedom (ie, delivery), let me out, let me out! Stimulated by the music, the beat, and the rocker's voice and body movements, the fans relive in fantasy their unconsciously

remembered emotional peaks and nadirs from the ambivalently benign/oppressive late-stage womb and birth.

The fans are engaged in struggle as they respond to the rocker's call, as they would to a preacher's call, to be born again.

Much rock music tells of that struggle, for it is replete with analogic material relating to the pre-natal drama, to the struggle of the foetus to gain liberation from the asphyxiating womb. The yearning to flee from the threats of external reality to a fantasised comfortable womb is powerful, and some music can pander to the wish, but most rock contains the reminder that the womb's attraction may lure the listener into a trap; the sought-after peace will be reached only in Nirvana. The gynaecological fact is that the foetus lives in a world of pain as well as pleasure and the ultimate price for the foetus is to die or to get out. Rock is an incitement: let me out and be born anew.

For the young, therefore, rock can act as a liberation, affording the gain of a second chance, providing an opportunity to start again and, in androgynous state, hold sexual and gender identity in suspense before the final decisions are taken, adolescence left behind, and adulthood reached; it is a case of *reculer pour sauter*. Even if a grown-up man may playfully indulge himself in an occasional dalliance with rock, to be seriously 'into' rock in your 40s is surely an arrest, not a hobby.

To find such a man in the rôle of a political leader places one on enquiry. Why, so persistently, does Blair immerse himself in this born-again world of rock, the world without commitment, of gender disorientation, of sexual nomads, of the Rolling Stones, who, in their restless name, enshrine rock's stance? What is the need for this man to enter into the trance-inducing rock where, as in the Stones' 'Prodigal Son', the hero whose prototype is the footloose rebel of the biblical legend, rejects, as rock music critic Simon Frith has explicated, 'the constant behavioural calculus and moral accounting of settled existence, makes up his life as he goes along' and lives for the Now and the

New? Why is he so gripped by a medium which above all else is a manifestation of the fantasy of rebirth, the myth of regeneration?

And, most importantly and relevantly, are the politics of Blair only one more displacement of the symptoms so exotically displayed in his love affair with rock? The answer is chasteningly clear: his much-publicised involvement with rock should be regarded as a meretricious advertisement, a trailer, inviting the Labour Party and the nation to join him in an unbecoming adolescent dream of new regenerative politics. Only the deaf and the insensitive could have failed to hear the rock beat from the moment Blair commenced his address at the 1995 Labour Party conference. Repetitively deploying, like a vulgar stage hypnotist, staccato invocations or commands, in language drenched in birth imagery, he sought to lure us into his reverie:

> Today I place before you my vision of a new Britain.
> A nation reborn. Prosperous, secure, united. One Britain.
> New Labour. New Britain.
>
> I know that for some of you, New Labour has been painful. There is no greater pain to be endured in politics than the birth of a new idea.

And as he began, so he concluded:

> New Labour. New Britain. The party renewed. The country reborn. New Labour. New Britain.

Roll on, Blair. Have your photo-ops, as in the February 1996 issue of the music magazine *Q*, clad in Next with Cherie in Versace, sharing a fruit bowl with the Prince of Protean Perversity, sometime saluter of the Nazi flag, David Bowie, each of you, politician and rock star, flaunting your androgynous qualities, singing your bewildered androgynous anthem, expressing the dilemma whether these days boys or girls should be liked, which invokes moondust to dissipate confusions.

Rock on, Blair, with the moondust and with the kids. But count me and Old Labour out.

Blair's Palingenetic Myth

Everyone knows, since he never ceases to tell us, that Tony Blair is the most Christian of socialists; and he can claim that under his leadership there has been a phenomenal membership growth in the Christian affiliate organisations of the Labour Party. There is no novelty, of course, in having in the party leaders who claim that their Christianity informs and is indeed the source of their political commitment. In my lifetime I have known and often fruitfully worked with men from Stafford Cripps to George Thomas, Viscount Tonypandy, whose religious faith has been the dynamic behind their good works as politicians.

Harold Wilson, indeed, always peddled the view that the Labour Party owed more to Methodism than to Marxism; that may, however, be a hyperbolic claim. From Ernie Bevin and Aneurin Bevan to Michael Foot, the party has had as leaders determined secularists. In South Wales, when I entered the Commons, there were probably as many Labour MPs who fiercely derided the chapel as there were those who found their politics in its tenets. Sometimes these neighbouring secularist MPs of mine would publicly demonstrate their contempt for

Christianity. On civic Sundays, in accordance with the valley traditions which I too observed, the local MP would lead, together with the mayor, a march throughout the township preceded by brass bands and followed by the Red Cross, the Boy Scouts, the Territorials and members of the local voluntary organisations. The march always ended in the chapel for a civic service but at the entrance to the chapel these MPs, having endorsed the values of civic virtues, would ostentatiously bid their constituents goodbye and refuse to partake of 'the opium of the masses'. It was indeed amongst such secularist MPs that I found my firmest allies when all the churches of Britain, unitedly and in concert, sought in 1963 to sabotage my original efforts to reform the divorce laws.

Nevertheless, overall, the record shows that a particular exegetical theme has played a large part in the shaping of the political thought of many Labour leaders. It was one that perhaps owed more to the Old Testament than to the New, for the emphases and goals in early Judaism were always defined in terms of a collectivity; so that in the Prophets you will find no clear ideal of personal immortality or reward and punishment after death. The highest aim, particularly of early Judaism, was a collective aim and individual salvation was relegated to the concerns of the nation and the whole human race. Labour leaders, exposed to such an ethos in their upbringing, often transposed the notion of the priority of the collective good to their secular politics; and, much diluted, we find it echoed in Blair's rodomontade, which is so frequently permeated with reference to 'communitarianism'.

There is, therefore, no novelty in a Labour leader claiming his politics of community are informed by Christian beliefs; but there is another exegesis of Christian doctrine which, in the hands of the power-seeking politician, can be both malevolent and an abuse of its original text. It can lead, as Blair has sought to do, to the almost blasphemous appropriation of the resurrection, the making of the ancient myth into a subtext of the New Labour Party manifesto. 'Easter,' Blair declared in

1996, 'a time of rebirth and renewal, has a special significance for me and, in a sense, my politics.' The myth of renewal and rebirth is a dangerous ploy to introduce into politics. It is the myth which some historians, notably Roger Griffin, have described as the palingenetic myth. Etymologically, the term palingenesis, deriving from *palin* (again, anew) and *genesis* (creation and birth), refers to the sense of a new start or regeneration after a phase or a crisis of decline. It is precisely that myth, when it has invaded the politics of twentieth-century Europe, notably in Nazi Germany, that has wreaked havoc. This is the myth which Blair acknowledges pervades his politics and which, once again, he spelt out when addressing a Labour Party conference in April 1995: 'Today a new Labour Party is being born. Our task now is nothing less than the rebirth of our nation. A new Britain. National renewal ... New Labour being born. The task of building new Britain now to come.'

The well-head of palingenetic myth is, of course, religious; and in Christianity the resurrection of Jesus Christ places one such myth at the very centre of the whole faith. Notions of metaphorical death and rebirth envelop the symbolism of baptism, communion and Easter celebrations, while generations of Christian mystics have elaborated intricate verbal, pictorial and ritual mythologies to invoke the reality of spiritual rebirth on a high plane of being after dying to the world of the flesh. The invocation of such myths in politics can, very exceptionally, be inspirational; but they can, and have been in my lifetime, utterly disastrous.

Only one previous Labour leader, and that was in the nineteenth century, has in his politics drawn upon the myth, and to compare Blair's impoverished presentations with the language and content of that leader's addresses, and to place them in the context of the period, brings a chastening recognition of the dangerous banalities of Blair's persuasions that we shall, under his leadership, be born again in a new Britain. Given Blair's unselfconsciousness, and his illiteracy in the field of Labour's history, it is unlikely that he is aware that the leader who used the palingenetic myth inspirationally was Old Labour's founding father, Keir Hardie, a man from whom Blair would decidedly wish to distance himself. Keir Hardie was brought up by his parents in a sternly rational creed of agnosticism; but, like Blair and at about the same age, at 21, in 1877, he was converted to Christianity. His conversion never led him to peddle pap or in any way to temper his belligerence. Conciliation and consensus were no part of the interpretation he placed upon his creed; he would have had no truck with the ecumenicalism Blair constantly preaches. When Hardie became the first and lone socialist MP in the Commons, he flayed the churches for their neglect of the issue of unemployment and, when he addressed the congress of the Congregational Union of England and Wales in 1883, his speech caused uproar. He declared:

> Christianity today lay buried, bound up in the cerements of a dead and lifeless theology. It awaited a decent burial, and they in the Labour movement had come to resuscitate the Christianity of Christ, to go back to the time when the poor should have the Gospel preached to them, and the Gospel should be good news of joy and happiness in life ... Ring out the darkness of the land, ring in the Christ that is to be.

The delegates to the congress were outraged, but as Hardie's biographer comments, to nascent socialists and to radicals 'he seemed the Messiah of a new faith destined to regenerate mankind'. Such impossible regeneration was not to be, but more than any other man he was the maker of the Labour Party that Blair would now consign to the dustbin of history. Not without resistance, some of us succeeded in having a commemorative bronze head of Keir Hardie placed in the Palace of Westminster. As Labour MPs, panting for future Blairite patronage, leave the Chamber to enter the dining-room, they must pass the corner where he gazes upon them. There they would be wise to pause and see if they can dare to look him in the eyes.

Keir Hardie's use of the palingenetic myth was certainly not directed to immediate power-seeking in Parliament; he saw his rôle in the House as basically prophetic, with his eyes on a very distant future. He was a back-bench agitator who was not seeking to persuade his fellow-MPs but, rather, to address the voiceless masses outside the Commons in the slums and in the back-streets, and by his very detachment from the parliamentary games of his day, he was to beget an Independent Labour Party outside the House. His was no fantasy pregnancy, as is Blair's; his birthing was authentic.

When, however, Blair declaims national renewal and regeneration, he skates on very thin ice. We have had once before in twentieth-century Britain a party emphasising above all else its pristine nature. It was the New Party founded by the extraordinary and dangerous Oswald Mosley; it was a party that soon glided into overt fascism. More than 60 years ago, in Pontypridd, South Wales, I well recall how only a posse of miners protected me from the menacing thugs approaching me as, from the floor, I challenged the eloquent call of Mosley for national rebirth and regeneration. Mosley's fascism, its essential homogeneity, resided in its mythic call; and no one who ever heard him could doubt that he used it to powerful effect.

Mosley's fascism was a British outcrop of what Roger Griffin, in his painstaking survey of the nature of fascism throughout Europe, describes as 'generic fascism'; and he identifies the centrality of the palingenetic component of fascism's permanent mythic core to explain so much of its appeal. Repeatedly we have witnessed, during the Second World War, and in pre- and post-war Europe, the fascist vision of a new vigorous nation growing out of the destruction of an old system; and have seen how, given flawed leaders with an elective affinity to the psychological travail of their society, fascism has had the almost alchemical power to transmute black despair in their communities into a deluded and manic optimism which takes them along the road to self-destruction.

All these fascisms offered, and continue to proffer, regeneration; they promise to replace gerontocracy, mediocrity and national weakness with youth, heroism and national greatness, to bring into existence a New Man in an exciting new world in place of the senescent, played-out one that existed before. The vague or contradictory implications of the policies to realise such nebulous goals do not necessarily diminish their attraction, because it is precisely their palingenetic mythic power that matters, not their feasibility or human implications.

When, therefore, Blair, in October 1995, proclaimed, 'This is a new age, to be led by a new generation. I want this country to be young again', he induced a frisson in the politically informed remnant of my generation. We have heard that language before in the mouths of fascist demagogues. Blair's unbecoming adolescent dream of new regenerative politics acted out in rock may, although not without considerable misgivings, be tolerable, but when the dream of rebirth is elaborated into political manifestos proffering the elixir of youth, then we are placed on alert, for this was the poison offered by the Nazi and fascist hucksters and accepted by their dupes.

Politics smeared by the detritus of Nazi-fascist mythopoeia are themselves repellent. But, as Blair and his impertinent young political pups wage war on Old Labour, there are particular reasons why we should scoff at their claims that only a 'new generation' can save us. In their trepidation, as they seek to kill off the fathers, these political adolescents boost themselves with a dangerous amnesic and, thus drugged, the courageous youngsters, manned with piss-proud erections, dare to obliterate the reality that the most radical and 'regenerative' Labour government, that brought us the welfare state, was led by old men, by a cabinet of 20 men and women whose average age when they took up office was 61.65 years. That cabinet had come to power after a war in which Britain, led by an old man of almost 70, had successfully defied Nazi Germany, whose people, deluded by their cult of youth and their version of the palingenetic myth, believed themselves invincible.

Born two years after Attlee's governments had run their course, Blair irreverently brings no recall of the war and the immediate post-war years. His is to be the first not the second coming. With messianic pretensions, and with blatant narcissism, he would like us to believe his birth day heralded the coming, in the imminent millennium, of the generation that under his apostolic leadership would create a new Britain made in his image; and in his 'new age' we will be young again. In pursuit of that theme no cabinet of Blair's is to have older MPs; in the shadow cabinet reshuffle of 1995, older members, sometimes of considerable quality, were dismissed and Blair's office made it clear to capable others outside the shadow cabinet but just past the age of 55 that they could not look forward to ministerial status. In May 1996 leaders of 18 prominent UK business organisations, led by the Bank of England, joined forces to promote the value to business of mixed-age workforces, attracting and retaining experienced employees regardless of age; but Blair is determined no such mix will prevail in his cabinet.

Probably as a second son with an able older brother, now a successful QC with an expertise in banking law, displaced sibling rivalry plays its part in Blair's pushing aside of older members, MPs who could be much-needed anchormen in his future government. Certainly the scar of being known at his private school as Blair II may well not have healed. But it is his own narcissism, and his envelopment in the rhetoric of his palingenetic myth, that, fundamentally, prevents him from empathising with the elderly and which causes, unusually, his opportunism to fail him. Ignoring the electoral dangers of estranging voters who form an increasingly large section of the population, he is flagrantly corroborating ageism. Apotheosising the new, eulogising the young, means denigration of the old. He has ample precedent. Seen at its worst and most evil, the politics of regeneration and the homosexual ideal of virile young men found its full expression in Nazi Germany; there the 'unproductive' elderly, dubbed senile, came under the shadow of Hitler's euthanasia programme. But there are other ways of destroying the elderly than sending them to gas chambers.

One of them is to create a political ethos which by exclusion demeans them. There is an inherent sickness in a dogma which overvalues youth, denies its biological concomitant, immaturity, and, by insisting government must be informed by a scale of values where to be young is the ideal, inflames intergenerational rivalry. That, as the European Commission insists in its realistic report of March 1996 on the ageing of Europe, is precisely what is to be avoided if the Continent's demographic problems are not to result in disaster: 'There can be no doubt that the principle of solidarity between generations will emerge as a key factor in the adjustments which will have to be made.' But when Blair avows he intends to make Britain young again, he is spelling out, in an assault on the parental generation, his own unresolved Oedipal antagonism. And the very absurdity of his intent exposes its irrationality.

The demographic reality is that Britain will never be younger; our ageing is for ever. Compounding the birth rates of the 1920s and 1930s, lower than they had ever been before, is a whole range of factors – the pill, the sustaining range of advances in medical knowledge, feminism, increased male sterility – all guaranteeing that our low-fertility and low-mortality population cannot be magically conjured away by political incantations. The present British population contains far and away the oldest body of persons which has ever occupied our islands; and the position is irreversible.

It has been said that ageism, as a specifically social pathology, is an identifiable characteristic of late-twentieth-century society in advanced countries; certainly consumerism and its accompanying meretricious advertising industry deliberately inciting or encouraging all to be self-regarding and, by artifice and fashion, to be ever young, are a fertile field for the growth of ageism. Reminders, within such an environment, of the inevitability of ageing are increasingly unwelcome; the aged become disliked for, of course, dislike of the old is hatred of the self, the rejection of what one must become.

How such ageism disagreeably invades politics was unpleasantly illustrated in February 1996 when the Tory government deliberately sabotaged a most modest Private Members' Bill which sought to prevent upper age limits in job advertising; and although in the debate the Blairite front-bench spokesman promised 'comprehensive legislation to make age discrimination in employment illegal', albeit subject to 'consultation', his awareness of the consequences of present demographic changes and future technology did not bring any detailed pledges, any detailed thought-through responses, telling us how it is proposed to bring about the reordering of the whole working relationship which, in the face of the radically altered age composition of our country, has become an imperative.

Very much more is required than age discrimination legislation and attempts, outside the context of Britain's burgeoning employment problems, to take limited action to assist the jobless half of all men over 55, will be of little avail, for they are but a small part of a huge problem. In fact, as the 1996 Rowntree Foundation report shows, there are already today 7 million people of working age who have no jobs. Certainly political attitudes which treat ageing as a well-nigh intractable 'problem' and which implicitly suggest that the most that can be done is to assess what the narcissistic young can be persuaded to forfeit for the benefit of those who cannot look after themselves, those who have to live in institutions and those about to die are wholly defeatist. A striking proof of the political attitudes presently adopted is to be seen in the candidates' standard visit during an election campaign to a sheltered housing complex or a residential care home, a practice to which I plead guilty and which encourages the illusion that old age is little more than an object of welfare and that it is in such venues one finds the old – when the reality is that in my former constituency, as in most areas, 96 per cent of older people live in ordinary housing. Instruments which have been created to meet these chronic problems of ageing are not able to provide us today with the policies or actions required for the increasingly great majority of elderly people who present no 'problem' at all. But

we shall have little hope of converting into legislation
imaginative political thought directed to aid a society where
birth rates diminish, infant mortality has practically dis-
appeared, and longevity prevails, if the leader of the major
reforming party seems, judging by his language, himself
possessed by the Dorian Gray syndrome, the denial of the ageing
process and the eulogising of youth. In *The Picture of Dorian
Gray*, Wilde wrote:

> For there is such a little time that your youth will last –
> such a little time. The common hill flowers wither but
> they blossom again. The laburnum will be as yellow next
> June as it is now. In a month there will be purple stars on
> the clematis, and year after year the green night of its
> leaves will hold its purple stars. But we never get back
> our youth. The pulse of joy that beats in us at 20
> becomes sluggish ... Youth! Youth! There is absolutely
> nothing in the world but youth!

The brilliant narcissist's erotic worship of youth, however
mortified, is a destructive and threatening doxology, if, under
Blair, it is added to Labour's canon. For such evocations
prejudice efforts to bring about the necessary reordering of the
working lives of all who wish and are capable of employment, a
reordering which indeed is a prerequisite, despite rising
national income, if we are not to live in a country where an
increasing and substantial minority suffer severe social
disadvantage as unemployment grows in homes where no one at
all is in paid work.

To speak of making Britain young again is therefore a
dangerous evasion of the challenge that demographic and
technological changes now set us. Worse, importing such a
vocabulary into political discourse compounds the very problem
it is claiming to resolve; 'senile', 'geriatric', along with many
adjectives, as Peter Laslett in his constructive works on ageism
has long since pointed out, although originally quite innocent of
an insulting meaning, are now standard epithets of abuse. Such

pejorative views demean the elderly and are part of the stereotyping process by which attributions can be given to each and every member of an older generation, even although they are applicable only to an afflicted minority. Possessed by his palingenetic myth, Blair, not content with denigrating Old Labour, must depict Britain itself as age-encumbered; despite having spent three of the first and, as for all of us, perhaps the most formative five years of his life in Australia, no affectionate evocations of the Old Country come from Blair. Always he repeats his mantra, New Britain, New Labour, all must be young, neoteric and pristine. Blair, in these declarations, is neurotically displaying what Jung has termed the *puer aeternus* (eternal youth) syndrome, in which the individual refuses to accept his own mortality; ageing and finitude are denied, a notion highly acceptable to an electorate increasingly doubtful that eternity is to be found in a heavenly afterlife.

In political terms, to sustain such conceits means nothing must ever be seen to be stale; ripeness, maturity, are menacing. Blair's *doppelgänger* Peter Mandelson in press interviews defends notions of permanent revolution, of constant and never-ceasing questioning of the present. Modernity for the Blairites has long since ceased to be a means to the political end of facing the electorate with internal structures brought up to date; it has become doctrine. As Charlotte Raven, in her November 1995 *Observer* article, insightfully commented:

> ... modernisation, that procedural strategy turned pseudo-philosophy, is quietly becoming a doctrine. Under Kinnock's custodianship, you felt that it was genuinely the means to a proper political end. But then, having done all its work within the party, it should, logically, have evolved and been replaced by a concern with *what to do* with the success it was supposed to facilitate. Instead it has stretched its neck wider ... It is no more the conveyance, but the destination – the route map which has ended up at the Grail. And, scariest of all,

they've started to believe in it – as if *it* was ever anything at all.

An ageing Mao almost wrecked his country with a cultural revolution in which everything old and traditional was to be destroyed; his denial of approaching death was projected on to society which, at his command, was to be born anew, and thus he fantasised he too could will himself to be young again. We, of course, are in no danger of Blair's born-again farrago inflicting Mao-like turmoil upon us. His psyche is too striated with inhibitions compelling him at all costs to avoid serious conflict. Sensing the fatal flaw, this incapacity for action to correspond with his doctrine, Raven, quoting Blair's 'I want us to be young again', pertinently adds: 'If the modernisers' case signifies anything, it's this semantic incoherency, nostalgia for a future which they wish for but cannot create.'

The history of the British Labour movement provides us with few examples of leaders afflicted with this psychological flair; but there have, however, been not a few of this genre, into which Blair chasteningly fits, among past European socialist leaders who, more burdened than British leaders by ideology, usually with some version of Marxism, made strikingly visible, when in office, their total incapacity to match political action with their political theory.

The classical example, often cited, is Otto Bauer, one-time Austrian Foreign Secretary and leader of the Austrian socialist party, whose theorising so entranced Léon Blum that, when Bauer died in exile, Blum, as French prime minister, had him buried with all the ceremony of a state funeral. Freud had treated Bauer's father and then, aware of the bizarre family background, by unravelling the perplexities of Bauer's sister, discovered the aetiology of hysteria. Otto Bauer's own hysterical personality shaped his seductive and dangerous political style; it was a style which proved fateful to Austrian democracy, combining as it did a militancy of language with an almost total absence of deeds. As Blair, possessed by a palingenetic myth which is turning into a governing political doctrine, notoriously evades committing himself to legislative details telling how his doctrine would be applied, we are uncomfortably reminded of characters like Otto Bauer.

These reminders become even more insistent when one notes the conclusions of clinicians, like the American Alan Krohn, who have provided us with modern definitions, wrested from their clinical work, of the hysterical personality. Such a personality, it is suggested, may be something of a pace-setter:

> Though the hysteric remains within the bounds of convention, his sensitivity to the ambience of his culture makes him sensitive to emerging cultural trends just before they enter the main stream of the social ethos. In art, sports and popular intellectual pursuits, and even more in such visual, exhibitionistic areas as fashion, interior decorating and cocktail-party conversation, the hysteric frequently allies himself with what is coming into vogue ... the hysteric promotes modest, minor change that rarely challenges anything basic to the society. The changes they respond to and try to be early participants in are more of style than of ideology, though ... the former has at times tried to pass as the latter. The hysteric, in his excitement and participation in changes of style, can help a society foster the illusion of change, promoting a sense of self-satisfaction that things are moving ahead, without really disrupting and reconstructing anything important. These changes which the hysteric is inclined to usher in need not necessarily be completely trivial. However, even if the changes have substance the hysteric will strive to embody them only if their divergence from what has come before is slight. The hysteric enjoys change, but only as he enjoys sexuality – to flirt with it but to remain safe from it ...

Such observations are made after explorations of the early family experiences of those displaying these traits, experiences which can be found to be suggestive of the impingements within Blair's early environment. Certainly one persistent strand in the cluster of behaviour patterns which marks out the hysterical personality is the failure, after engagement in heavy petting with the Idea, to proceed to consummation.

And consummation of Blair's Idea seems to be ever postponed. Only on rare occasions out of the mist of his mythopoeic doctrine does any detailed proposal emerge; and even when it does, it too often seems to be juvenilia rather than serious and considered draft legislation. One such proposal, illustrative of the political pathogen carried by the Blairites, has come from Blair's close associate Peter Mandelson, the one-time active Young Communist fiercely defending Brezhnev's invasion of Czechoslovakia and a man whose present crusade against those he suspects of Old Labour tendencies always reminds me of a converted Revivalist warning against all the sins of which he has grown tired. One of his sudden conversions as a young man, after a short sojourn in Tanzania, where he appears to have found God, was from Marxism to Christianity; his belated conversion presumably lingers on in the proposal he has put forward, in an uncomfortable moralistic guise, for a public dowry to be made available to those committing themselves to permanent cohabitation with a partner. Proposals of this nature have a long and disreputable tradition and are unpleasantly reminiscent of right-wing, neo-fascist or fascist policies, where preoccupation with the need for national regeneration meant that population and family policies were ever conjoined.

France, even before Pétain, in 1939, had a revised *Code de la Famille* which enshrined, in laws which encouraged marriage and provided subsidies, the traditional apprehension that France's national grandeur would be subverted by under-population. In Italy Mussolini's regime was indeed founded on a palingenetic vision; the dictator's pronouncement as he denounced falling birth rates included constant mention of a 'spiritual renewal' of the Italian people, and the 'rebirth' of a 'young and fertile race' the delivery of which he sought to facilitate by subsidies rewarding prolific women for performing their patriotic service to the nation. And in some ways, in Nazi Germany, Mandelson's dowry scheme was pre-empted. Side by side with an evil 'eugenic' programme aimed to ensure a rebirth of an Aryan race, purified of tainted blood, came incitements to the racially pure to increase their numbers. The Nazis were particularly proud of their marriage loans system. The Nazi scheme gave couples interest-free loans of up to 1,000 marks the repayment of which was cancelled when they had their fourth child. Issued in the form of coupons for household goods, the loans were initially given on condition that the future wife who had worked for at least six months prior to the wedding gave up gainful employment after marriage.

Mandelson's dowry scheme is, however, not a copycat of the Nazi dowry system. That scheme is to be differentiated from Mandelson's in the method used to finance its cost; inspired by French legislation, the fund to pay the loan was partly financed by the revenue from a 'celibacy tax' on unmarried men and women, a method of fund-raising which would certainly not be personally advantageous to bachelors like Mandelson. His method of fund-raising is far less equitable, and it is one that unsurprisingly emerges from the youth culture that the palingenetic mythology corroborates. He would urge a form of generational tax law on 'empty nesters' in their 60s who, having worked for decades to rid themselves of their mortgage are, he complains, enjoying 'reasonable incomes with low outgoings' and 'are sitting on significant equity capital' which should be mobilised 'to give young people a better start to married life'. This man, lacking in-laws and children, would have legislation creating the flexibility to release this equity, legislation which will be clearly seen to all but those lacking sensibility to provoke guilt or resentments if the parents failed to take advantage of its provisions.

There are other peculiarities about Mandelson's scheme. All the neo-fascist and Nazi family funding schemes had a clear and unequivocal goal: young marriages meant more births and thus assisted national regeneration. Mandelson, perhaps embarrassed by his lack of marital status, is less explicit, but birth production, nevertheless, is part of the goal of his dowry plan; it would 'make life with a new baby so much more bearable' and, he claims, the dowry would reduce 'the anxiety, frustration and tension at a testing moment in any relationship'. Parenthood seems to be viewed by this man not as a blessing, as I have certainly experienced it, but, if not a curse, certainly a penalty which a state-endowed dowry should mitigate. It is a view which is not out of kilter with his ambivalence about marriage itself, for that is not presented as a good in itself but merely a useful indicator, affording 'the simplest test of eligibility' for the dowry; and in his book, as in his surrounding interviews, he looks forward to the proposal being extended 'to couples who affirm a long-term commitment to each other but for reasons of their own reject the form of marriage'. In his order, homosexuals in long-term relationships and cohabiting heterosexuals should, ideally, not be excluded; and, more, to further the overall scheme, the old should pay for all this by tightening inheritance taxes.

That so jejune a scheme, one replete with generational bias, so likely to attract mercenary and unstable couples and so calculated to provoke resentment, as qualification for the dowry would bring financial means tests and evaluations of permanent 'commitment' by bureaucrats, is seriously put forward by someone so close to Blair is dismaying. Most of my parliamentary life was spent in reforming laws impinging upon human relationships, and I know how delicately one must tread if, in the end, such legislation is to be healing, not disruptive. But even if one discounts some of the personal dilemmas that are reflected in Mandelson's inept proposal, this whole ill-thought-out notion remains unhappily illustrative of the Blairite's fatal attraction to the inchoate; always the canvassing of an alleged new Idea, never the detailed signposting of the route to its fulfilment.

The malaise afflicts so many of their proposals, be they for devolution, for public ownership of the railways or for reform of the House of Lords. What we are firmly and repetitively told is that Blair stands for the future, a future which he has made into a proposal in itself; and this future, reborn Britain, will come about like a happening, and only the querulous and unimaginative spread their doubts about the efficacy of this spell within his palingenetic myth-making. And these dissenters can be dealt with by the leader's speech being accompanied by a briefing for journalists stating the New Initiatives catalogued in his address, notably 'a new type of politics, no promises which we cannot deliver'. So the future will come about with the new promise, a promise not to promise, an innovatory and brave pre-election pledge calculated to lend an air of credibility and realism to his fantasy.

But such a political environment beckons in disenchantment, for, ultimately, government by dream will collide with reality. The creation of this political environment has, however, more immediate effects; it not only incites ageism but it sabotages the constructive work of those like Peter Hildebrand, the psychoanalyst who for 20 years conducted at the Tavistock Clinic a workshop on the problems of the second half of life. Rebelling against the oppression of the predominant youth culture which Blair's political expositions reinforce, it is possible to see ageing as a creative process, not as an arrest, in the course of which, despite having to cope with new pressures on relationships, as well as old conflicts, and despite increasing physical limitations, rich and fulfilling possibilities are offered for exploration and discovery of the latent and unfulfilled aspects of ourselves.

The years between the early 40s and old age should not be regarded as a mere postscript; to do so at a time when the post-parental phase of robust health has been so greatly extended, and when for the first time men and women can look forward to 30 to 50 years of productive life after their children have reached adulthood, is, when expressed by Blair in his paeans of praise for the new and young, wholly inappropriate to today's societal needs and is as presumptuous as it is destructive.

Blair's belated religious instruction apparently did not include the importance of obeying the Fifth Commandment.

The deficit in Blair's programme is the lack of wisdom; he accelerates the change that has taken place in recent decades – the abandonment of the wisdom of the elders and their capacity to make a worthwhile contribution. The pace of technological change, leaving so many older people feeling they are immigrants in a strange land, encourages the notion that they are to be regarded as surplusage; but the Internet provides information, not wisdom. I am only too conscious as I approach my 80th birthday of how the raw speed and effectiveness of much of the thinking of the young, as part of the natural process, decline with age; but this is often amply compensated for in the ageing individual by the capacity to scan the field and arrive at solutions by using a process of lateral thinking, a capacity that tends to evolve in response to the gradual and sometimes imperceptible losses in the ageing process.

Hildebrand has neatly illustrated this trend in telling of that brilliant tactical thinker the first Duke of Wellington. When the Great Exhibition was opened, the vast Crystal Palace was plagued with a completely unforeseen infestation of the common London sparrow, which threatened to lay a thin layer of mess and untidiness over the whole sparkling edifice and its contents. Those responsible for the Exhibition were close to despair, with the result that Queen Victoria decided to consult the Duke, who was then in his 80s and regarded by her as the repository of all wisdom. On this occasion his tactical genius gave her the immediate and sensible answer that Prince Albert and the scientists and engineers had not been able to discern: 'Sparrow-hawks, Ma'am. Sparrow-hawks.' The Duke had seen through to the heart of the problem and found the answer which had escaped the scientists.

If the maximum available benefit is to be obtained by our society, then the zeal and energy of the young need to be tempered by those whose age often brings them greater detachment, a talent to stand back from the fray, above the immediate battle, and enables them to bring a sense of balance and authority. It is a need that exists in the boardroom, in the deliberations of trade union executives and university councils, and most obviously in our politics now so replete with a sense of expediency forever practised on a day-to-day level. It is because Blair senses the growing public distaste for this present form of government, its venality matching its opportunism and desperate improvisations, that he claims he is bringing a 'new type of politics'; what in fact he proffers is the oldest type of politics: the politics of the shaman whose magic the credulous believed could control good and evil and whose incantations could quicken the dead. But there is no dodging ageing and death; and no one and no nation can be born again.

Even as age cannot long be disguised by cosmetic and surgeon, so too the politics of the pristine, of the new, cannot long be sustained; its blemishes will soon emerge. Mature democracies and older people alike must accept their losses. In Britain's case, its loss of empire and military and economic power has to be mourned even as a once-beautiful woman must mourn. Recapturing youth is a foolish and vain quest and it is irresponsible to plead, as Blair is doing in political terms, its possibility.

There are more positive responses open to ageing; and if those responses infuse the body politic, as can occur through more emotionally mature leadership, then out of the acknowledgement of loss and out of the mourning, there can come a creative liberation. George Pollock, the American analyst who has contributed much to an understanding of the potentiality of ageing, has spelled out what he has called the mourning-liberation process:

> The basic insight is the parts of the self that once were, or
> that one hoped might be, are no longer possible. With
> the working out of the mourning for a changed self, lost
> others, unfulfilled hopes and aspirations, as well as
> feelings about other reality losses, there is an increasing

ability to face reality as it is and as it can be. 'Liberation' from the past and the unattainable occurs. New sublimations, interests and activities appear. There can be new relationships with old internal objects as well as new objects. Past can truly become past, distinguished from present and future. Affects of serenity, joy, pleasure and excitement come into being. Narcissism may be transformed into humour, wisdom and the capacity to contemplate one's one impermanence.

Pollock may be too optimistic, and the ideal he claims is possible may only rarely be achieved; but it is a goal that can be set before a society as before an individual, and the politician, like Nye Bevan, who never ceased to affirm that the achievement of societal serenity was the purpose of his politics, had an understanding of the developmental process that can operate in the body politic. Anabolic and catabolic forces are forever driving within our society, and which of these competing forces triumph is extraordinarily dependent upon the available leadership. When Blair discards and mocks Old Labour, and invites us to become engulfed within his palingenetic myth, he is retreating from adult politics; youth is a beginning not an end, and to make, within our politics, by sound-bite, posture and sloganising posters, an apotheosis of all that is young and new is both dangerously regressive and pusillanimous. Technology and demography ensure that never in British history has there been a greater need to capture the courageous mood, so unlike Blair's, of Robert Browning; it is the mood which is required to envelop our politics:

> Grow old along with me
> The best is yet to be
> The last of life for which the first was made.
> Our times are in His hand
> Who saith, A whole I planned.
> Youth shows but half; trust God; see all; be not afraid.

The Hermaphrodite and the Androgynous: The Distinction

Blair lures the voters even as did the Pied Piper of Hamelin, who cheated the spellbound children of their adulthood and led them back into the womb-mountain, for the leadership that Blair provides is that of androgyny, one that infantilises the electorate; its identity is vague, ill-defined and free from the burden of adult and gender choice.

If we are to be alerted to the hazards such political leadership provides, then we must discern the distinction between the debased charisma it exudes, one to which a confused and immature electorate responds, and the charisma of leaders, of whom Gaitskell and Bevan are contemporary British examples, possessed of hermaphrodite charm. Even a slight excursus into the history of the influences exercised by hermaphrodite leaders and myths illuminates how different is their spell from that exercised by the androgynous, and how each spell can have entirely different political consequences.

The prototype of all those exercising hermaphrodite

leadership is to be found in the man who is so often described as the first individual in history, the Pharaoh Akhenaten, living 14 centuries before Christ, a ruler who in all the various images exhumed by the archaeologists is depicted as effeminate, lacking a phallus or, more usually, with an explicit hermaphrodite anatomy. When, as in the Royal Academy's African art exhibition of 1996, we are left only with a remnant of this extraordinary leader which is confined to his face, still we are ensnared by his seductive and sensuous lips, as we may well be, for he has, as no other man, captured the imagination of the most austere of Egyptologists, as well as men like Freud, who regard him as perhaps the greatest man that has ever lived. The revered Egyptologist James Breasted wound up his classic study of Akhenaten's reign in these words:

> There died with him such a spirit as the world had never seen before – a brave soul, undauntedly facing the momentum of immemorial tradition, and thereby stepping out from the long line of conventional and colourless pharaohs, that he might disseminate ideas far and beyond the capacity of his age to understand. Among the Hebrews, seven or eight hundred years later, we look for such men; but the modern world has yet adequately to value or even acquaint itself with this man who in an age so remote and under conditions so adverse, became not only the world's first idealist and the world's first *individual*, but also the earliest monotheist, and the first prophet of internationalism – the most remarkable figure of the Ancient World before the Hebrews.

The typology of Akhenaten has thrown attempted medical diagnoses of his physical condition into confusion. The assertion that he suffered from a disorder of the endocrine system, that there was a malfunction of the pituitary gland, and that the indications are that the peculiar physical characteristics which all his depictions reveal are the result of a complaint known as Fröhlich's syndrome, have been subverted by the fact that

Akhenaten, uniquely among the pharaohs in having himself represented as a family man, seldom appears except in the company of his wife and daughters. The physicians cannot resolve the dilemma: how can so uxorious a husband and so philogenetive a parent have suffered from Fröhlich's syndrome, which would have rendered him impotent and passive except for a short period in adolescence before the full onset of the disease?

Perhaps Akhenaten did have some physical characteristics suggestive of the hermaphrodite, but the manner in which he directed himself to be depicted, where all such characteristics are heavily emphasised, sometimes to the point of caricature, sometimes grotesquely, clearly meant he was determined that his self-perception and his people's perception of him should be that of a leader possessed of the powers of the hermaphrodite; those powers he exercised in a staggering manner against the Egyptian establishment and priesthood, precipitating a revolution in thought, notably in his insistence on monotheism, that reverberates down the ages. Indeed, if Freud's conjecture in the most arresting of all his works is correct, the original Moses was himself an Egyptian follower of Akhenaten.

What is clear beyond peradventure is that the later chroniclers, in the biblical Books of Moses, had wholly absorbed, in telling of the god of the Hebrews, the notion of an hermaphrodite organism which has explicitly male and female sexual reproductive characteristics; for woman as well as man, Genesis insists, was created in the image of the god who evidently contained both elements. And being so created, Eve springs from Adam's rib. This concept of a primal divine hermaphrodism, found of course in the creation account of so many cultures, arises from the wish to believe that the Ultimate Being is a unity in which all present pairs of opposites, including the sexes, were contained. Ancient myths abound in tales of a time when the eternal male, Father Sky, and the eternal female, Mother Earth, were locked in unending embrace; there was neither duality nor multiplicity, only one hermaphrodite condition. It was only later, when the cosmic egg was broken, that creation took place. The sexes were separated, and have ever since longed to be reunited, each in the other.

The Greeks, less coy than the Jews, were more explicit in telling of humankind's nostalgia for the once-upon-a-time when man and woman were one. In their art, as in the statues of the Graeco-Roman epoch, they often projected on to the mythological figures, whom they regarded as harbingers of their destiny, fully developed female bodies with pronounced male sex organs. Far from denying sexuality, such depictions emphasise its presence; we witness in the marble portrayals both the eternal wish expressed in the mythic idea that once man and woman were one, and an acknowledgement that all human beings are potentially bisexual. The hermaphrodite affirms sexuality and the dictionary definition of hermaphrodite, which presents androgyny as its equivalent, is misleading, for the androgynous, contrariwise, wishes to negate sexuality, to deny, by blurring, any gender whatsoever; male and female are to be neither separately defined nor explicitly conjoined.

In our present day, androgyny, as exhibited by our pop stars and fashion models, is a retreat from genitality, which is adult and carries therefore the threat of responsibility; however attractively displayed or packaged, retreat, defeat and deadness are endemic to its condition. In politics the charisma of the hermaphrodite leader can lead followers to catastrophe, but as a weapon in the hands of a leader retaining a firm hold on reality it can be inspirational, and a resultant benign dynamic can arise within his society. No such hope can be wrested from an androgynous leadership; the conservatism inherent in its nature, the ebb-tide ever dragging such a leader back to the magic islands, to the imagined security of the womb, overrides all the overdetermined protestations that, with him, we can face the future.

The terrible accusation that can be made against such a leader, far worse than any that can come from a ministerial front bench, is that involuntarily he is a practitioner of the politics of perversion; for politics too is an arena where, to a greater or lesser extent, perverse elements which may feature in the lives of people suffering from various forms of disturbance may be acted out.

Androgyny is a dangerous quality; by its very nature shirking full consummation, it sometimes expresses itself in perversions in the clinical sense, often finding the fetish more attractive and safer than the woman. A distinction, however, exists between the true pervert and those who, like the vast majority of people, from time to time indulge in fantasies, usually sexual, which deviate from the culturally accepted norms; indeed, for many of them the most they do is put their fantasies into occasional practice in their foreplay.

While the true pervert's deviance is a persistent and constant form of aberrant sexual behaviour, androgyny, carrying with it perverse elements, can pervade the global structure involving the individual's whole personality, and find its expression in activities which fall far short of, and are to be differentiated from, those which are correctly given the diagnostic designation of perversion. I believe Blair's politics to be riddled with such elements; and that the consequences of such politics to our society can be far more dangerous than the activities of the true wretched clinical pervert, often indulging his practices alone, and always confined to sexual deviance.

Politics of Perversion

To allege that we are being enveloped in the politics of perversion is a serious charge; and, if it is to be sustained, we must turn to the clinicians whose case-books bulge with the histories of perverts, and then ask whether our surmise is validated by their findings, and whether, without extravagances, we can suggest that in many respects the politics we are being invited to practise are analogous to the pervert's lifestyle, and stem from similar sources.

The task we set ourselves is fraught with difficulties, not least because of the disgust and outrage which can be provoked by the very mention of the word 'pervert'. Our protestations that we must always distinguish, as do the psychoanalysts, between true perverts and those who may show what is described by the psychoanalysts as 'sub-clinical perverse elements' in character structures are irrationally brushed aside. There comes into existence a quaint notion that psychiatric research into those elements should be based on the less prominent members of the human race, exempting the prominent, the great and the sublime. Such a reaction is understandable, as the tabloids daily confirm Schiller's poetic aside: 'The world loves to blacken the radiant and drag the sublime into the dust.' But a path can be steered between tabloid scavenging and, in the genuine public interest, a necessary scrutiny of our political leaders: 'There is no one so great,' Freud wrote when justifying his scrutiny of Leonardo da Vinci, 'as to be disgraced by being subject to the laws which govern both normal and pathological activity with equal cogency.'

There is a further difficulty, however, in surveying the operation of perverse elements in the politics of the leaders and the led. Perforce the starting-point of such a survey must be a search for the origins of the true pervert's startling deviations; and it is at first disconcerting to find that among those who have gained an expertise in the treatment of perverts there is a tendency, particularly as between psychoanalysts in Britain and those in France, to take up differing vantage points as they focus upon the first precipitates of a pervert's condition. All the psychoanalysts, however, share a common view that the bizarre practices of the pervert constitute a regressive attempt to shield himself from a reality that he finds too threatening to tolerate.

In Britain the emphasis of the psychoanalytically orientated psychiatrist is upon the stratagems that the pervert has invented to protect himself from the retaliatory action which he fears will be evoked because of his aggression, aggression which is at large and liable to bring about his annihilation. In France, psychoanalysts, and particularly the remarkable Janine Chasseguet-Smirgel, have a different focus. The disclosures of their patients have taught them that the pervert, fearful of further libidinal development that would take him into full genital relationships – which he regards as terrifyingly threatening – retreats from unbearable truth to find his shelter in practices which have an accompanying fantasy of a perverse world where orifices are indistinguishable, where there is no distinction between the vagina and the anus; it is the universal anal-sadistic world of the Marquis de Sade, an imagined world where all reality has been pounded into an undifferentiated non-threatening mass. There, the pervert, wallowing in this mire, opts to be bogged down rather than reach an adult world where, unlike in the pervert's fantasised world, differences between the sexes and generations prevail.

Neither British nor French analysts, however, in any way categorise the pervert's practices as conduct totally outside the range of experience known to most people; the British analysts stress that some of the pervert's longings can be a component of the most normal of loving desires, and Chasseguet-Smirgel sees perversions as 'a dimension of the human psyche in general, a temptation in the mind common to us all'. There is therefore substantial congruity between both viewpoints; and the clinical evidence yielded by both means that we can expect that perverse components within a political leader's propaganda can, at an unconscious level, find a resonance throughout the whole community. In my view, those resonances are being teased out by current presentations of Blairite policies within which we find distressing analogues of the desperate efforts of the pervert who gains, within the fantasies accompanying his tortuous practices, temporary relief from his anguish. To recognise those analogies, it is wiser to adopt the viewpoint of both schools of psychoanalysis separately, although, since both are based substantially on the bedrock of classical Freudian theory, doubtless at some future time the metapsychological theory may evolve harmonising their present differences.

Psychoanalysts in Britain who treat perverts have come to recognise a particularly important complex of interrelated feelings, ideas and attitudes which they refer to as the 'core' complex of perversion. Dr Mervin Glasser, the dedicated consultant psychiatrist who at London's Portman Clinic has treated so many perverts and who brings illumination to the nature of the complex, tells us:

> A major component of the core complex is a deep-seated and pervasive longing for an intense and most intimate

closeness to another person, amounting to a 'merging', a 'state of oneness', a 'blissful union' ... This longed-for state implies complete gratification with absolute security against any dangers of deprivation or obliteration and a totally reliable containment of any destructive feelings towards [the other person, usually the mother or mother surrogate].

The case histories Glasser uses to illustrate the components of the core complex have a familiar ring. When, for example, he tells us of a transvestite imagining himself crawling up the birth passage and curling up snugly within the womb, we note the correspondence between that fantasy and Blair's dream of a blissful union, of a politics without discordance or schism; and we note too how similar are the yearnings of the transvestite to those embedded in Blair's favourite rock music, which is replete with the bliss of an imagined pre-natal condition; and, no less, we see equivalences between the transvestite's 'merging' and the return to the womb which is the precondition for the fulfilment of the palingenetic myth governing Blair's politics.

But it is when we turn to the psychoanalyst's search for the origins of the true pervert's compulsive need to escape from reality, from the dangers he feels in the external world, that we begin to understand that the acts of the pervert are not what they seem to be, and that in most cases they conceal their real nature rather than reveal it; for the perversions and the accompanying fantasies are in place as a shield to protect him from the consequences of the unconscious violences which seize him and which, if released, would destroy him and others.

When we grasp what Edward Glover, the doyen of the last generation of British psychoanalysts, asserted – that the pervert's wayward behaviour is 'a defence against an overcharge of unconscious aggression and/or sadism' – then I believe we find lit up for us the darkest crevices of the perverse elements within Blairite politics. Blair's placatory style, his need to have consensus by *diktat*, his concentration on the 'middle ground' and his avoidance at all costs of 'extremism', his attempts to outlaw Old Labour, which insists that all the gains for ordinary people have come about, not by wooing, but by struggle and by fights which must be sustained, we begin to appreciate that his approach is determined by a force in respect of which electoral advantage is little more than justification for his own perverse political compulsions.

Always a distinction must be made between a true perversion and the perverse elements which may appear in the lives and ideologies of those to whom the diagnostic designation, with all its pejorative and sometimes criminal overtones, most certainly does not apply. But with that *caveat* again made and emphasised, I nevertheless believe that Blair's fear of political confrontation with anyone except those who would deny him consensus, can be understood better if we acknowledge that his fated mishandling of his own unconscious aggression is akin in some respects to what we see erotically endured by the true pervert.

When under Glover's chairmanship and tutelage I served for so many years on the council of the Institute for the Scientific Treatment of Delinquency, I needed no persuasion from him to accept his view that the perversions were indeed a defence against an overcharge of unconscious aggression, for as a newly qualified solicitor I had found myself not infrequently defending perverts who had offended against public order; and they had taught me what Glover explicated. I still recall my shock when, after successfully persuading the court to inflict a non-custodial sentence on a pervert and after, outside the court, I had counselled him to confine his practices to the private domain, he peremptorily walked away from me, saying he could not do that for, if he stopped, he would kill someone. A few years later I heard that in another city he was charged with attempted murder; his perversion, stifled or inadequately realised, had proved too frail to contain his violence.

On another occasion, by which time I had gained more professional experience, the replies I received when questioning a perverted murderer client about his motivation gave me less surprise. He was engaged in his perversions in a bath with his colluding wife when he suddenly desisted and proceeded to cut her up in little pieces. When I asked him, in his cell, why he had slain his wife, he replied tonelessly: 'I had to. If I hadn't killed her, I would have killed myself.' He was being truthful; the self-lacerations that he would have inflicted when even his perversions could not protect her from his aggression had been unleashed upon his wife. Such dramatic presentations of the link between unconscious aggression and perversion may only exceptionally come to the notice of a criminal lawyer, but they are evidently commonplace within the experience of clinicians. One psychoanalyst has written: 'When one works, as I do, psychotherapeutically with both delinquents and sexual deviants, one may observe how the patients may be graded on a continuum ranging from violence to true perversions. In some instances one may actually observe the process of sexualisation taking place before one's eyes, so to speak, in the course of the treatment.'

The terrible violences that can result when the barrier of the pervert's defences are breached must not, however, mislead us into believing that the true pervert is someone utterly different from ourselves, that he does not belong to the human race. He goes as a babe through the same developmental stages as we all do; but the tragedy of the pervert is that the dilemmas from which the majority of us escape, carrying only perverse elements of greater or lesser strength, remain raw and wholly dominant in the pervert's adult life.

The developmental stage of infant life in which the psychoanalysts tell us the adult pervert remains can, without, it is hoped, lapsing into excessive distortion or oversimplification, be succinctly depicted. Our initial intense need as babes for the mother creates a wish to merge with her, but that wish carries the implicit concomitant of the loss of a separate existence as an individual – annihilation. To avoid such a fate there is an intensive aggressive reaction aimed at self-preservation and the destruction of the mother; but such a destruction would lead to the loss of the mother, to total abandonment, so the babe's woes are compounded as the anxiety he felt that he would be annihilated by merger is now supplemented by his anxiety that he would be abandoned. The force of the aggression which he feels because he is thus trapped in an impossible dilemma is not to be minimised, and it is that aggression that we find can be released by the adult pervert who has never resolved the original Catch-22 situation.

Although the babe cannot extricate himself from the predicament, fortunately the mother can and does come to the rescue for most of us. It is her ministering to our needs that helps us on our way. Gradually, as her mothering endows us with the confident self and diminishes our fear of individuation, the wish to merge becomes less insistent. Gradually the confidence grows that the mother's temporary absence does not mean abandonment; and so, the fortunate babe's aggression is increasingly tempered and the consequent anxieties lessened.

The adult pervert, however, has not been so saved. The mothering he received was defective, and failed to resolve his dilemma. Glasser has authoritatively told us of the mothers who bequeath so wretched a legacy:

> Frequently we have no objective information to corroborate the patients' depiction of their mothers, but one characteristic features so consistently in the accounts the true perverts give that one is safe to assume their veracity. This is that she has a markedly narcissistic character and relates to her child in narcissistic terms ... Her narcissistic overattentiveness, in treating him as part of herself, reinforces his annihilatory anxieties and intensifies his aggression towards her. Her neglect, emotional self-absorption and insensitivity to her child's needs will both frustrate him and arouse abandonment anxieties and again intensify his aggression towards her.

The psychoanalyst categorises the characteristics of the mother who creates the true pervert, but even when the characteristics of the mother appear in less florid form, but when the mothering is less than good enough, then the imperfections that prevent the mother from empathising with the babe and adequately meeting his emotional needs mean that the babe, when he reaches adulthood, will be likely to have far more perverse elements within his psychic life than an adult whose infancy was happily blessed; and the most significant social consequence is that such an adult will have greater difficulty in handling his own aggressivity.

This is the handicap maiming Blair's politics. The true pervert is attempting to prevent his unconscious aggression surfacing, destructively imploding and exploding. By his sexual deviations he attempts to quench the annihilatory anxieties which came from the threat when he was a babe that his enveloping mother would fulfil his wish for merger, and his abandonment anxieties, which stem from his fear that the destruction he wished to wreak upon the narcissistic mother denying him individuation would leave him abandoned. However, a mothering less starved than one which results in the true pervert, but one which nevertheless is similar if less defective than such mothering, can result in an adult finding himself compelled, in self-protection, in a bid to keep under control the aggression which in more normal development may have been benignly assimilated, to use stratagems, albeit more subtle than the pervert's; and it is my view that Blair's consensus by *diktat* politics is such a stratagem.

Not for nothing is the gibe deservedly made against him as he seeks Conservative votes that he should be renamed 'Tory Blair'; he desperately needs his consensus, one from which aggression is proscribed and conflict banished, even as the true pervert needs his bizarre sexual deviations. Blair's biography, personal and political, tells us of a man struggling with unconscious and unassimilated aggression; but the consequent perverse elements are not expressed in sexual deviance. They are seen in his incapacity, like his mentor Macmurray, to tolerate ambivalence, in his constant display of rock-womb yearnings, in his immersion in the palingenetic myth. The impress of his mother's narcissism is as firmly delineated upon him as it is upon a true tragic pervert; and the perverse elements finding expression in his politics have a similar object as that of the true pervert, to hold down unconscious aggression which threatens to escape. That aggression in Blair's case has, through his traumatic early experiences, been repeatedly recharged and has constantly been stifled, not least during the period when his father, dead but alive, would look at his son with eyes which the boy would almost inevitably have regarded as accusatory.

There will be those who demur, and protest how can it be suggested, given the scant information available, that Blair's mother, although courageous, had in all probability a markedly narcissistic character and related to her baby in narcissistic terms; but the trained clinician treating his adult pervert usually and similarly lacks objective information to corroborate his patient's depiction of his mother. However, the clinicians have, by noting the common features of their pervert patients' depictions of their mothers, collected sufficient material to build up and to test their hypotheses and the validation of their hypotheses comes in the success or partial success of their therapy.

The therapist, it is true, has the advantage of the consulting-room or the couch; but Blair is no shrinking violet. Lacking reticence, this actor, composing his scripts or choosing those he finds congenial to his temperament, provides almost daily a plenitude of material unlikely to be so readily proffered by a patient to his therapist and, within that material, with a constant presentation of consensus politics, we see the same desperate urge to maintain psychic stability as possesses the pervert whose practices are *his* attempts to contain the violences which he fears would otherwise break out against himself or others.

Both the pervert and such politics are reaching out for what psychoanalysts have described as psychic homoeostasis, akin to the physiological concept of homoeostasis, the tendency of organisms to maintain themselves in a constant state. But the capacity of the individual to adapt to the demands and disturbances which arise from clamorous internal needs and from those made by the external world is profoundly affected by his earliest upbringing; and, handicapped by a particular upbringing, the pervert's mistaken efforts to achieve homoeostasis are wretched and precarious, and so are Blair's.

The precariousness of Blair's imperfect homoeostasis is reflected, in political terms, in his ceaseless efforts to impose a discipline upon his party members, to silence any who criticise his stances; for his psychic homoeostasis is fraught with all his primal and subsequent traumatic anxieties. By June 1996 the *Observer*, well primed by Blair's entourage, was able to report under the headline 'Blair tightens his grip on party':

> Labour MPs judged below standard or disloyal may be barred from standing as official candidates after the general election under new proposals to be canvassed by Tony Blair ... Labour's leader will also seek a tighter rein on parliamentary candidates by urging local parties to choose from a list drawn up by Labour's National Executive.

It is jejune of Hugo Young to attribute, as he does, Blair's 'iron hand' to a fear that any expressed dissension will be exploited by those manning a hostile media. Blair can and does accommodate them; he has no difficulty in having a *rapprochement* with Murdoch or lunches with the editorial staff of the *Sun*. What Blair fears is not the press but himself.

What Blair cannot accommodate is Old Labour's insistence that working strictly within the parameters of the prevailing economic system means Britain will never have the changes it needs. That is heresy, for acceptance of that doctrine would affect the consensus he has built up, one which, despite all the posturing and rhetoric, has left the electorate believing, on good grounds, that there are few policy differences between any of the political parties. It is a heresy which, if adopted, would upset Blair's precariously poised homoeostasis, one that is so brittle a container of his free-floating unconscious aggression. Traditional Labour is, therefore, more of a personal than a political threat to Blair; and because, fraught with anxiety, he finds it so threatening to his personal intactness, all his considerable unconscious aggression is released against those who show the slightest tendency to deviate from his contrived consensus. Then we see him as Robert Harris, the novelist and journalist, has described him: 'He is emerging as the most ruthless leader Labour has had, imposing a revolution on his party like Thatcher did on hers.'

But this is a 'revolution' to serve Blair's needs, not those of the party or the country. How compelling are those needs, and how near paranoiac Blair is in his concern that his homoeostasis remains in place, are shown in his new and elaborate plan to undermine the authority of the activists of the Labour conference by subjecting their decisions to the veto of all the more easily manipulated Johnnie-come-lately members, so many of whom have joined as a response to Blair's popular universally painless utterances. Too many of these members have not yet learned that authentic leadership does lead, not follow; no MP, whether back-bencher or leader, should act as a seismograph passively registering the temporary prejudices of the electorate. No promised land will be reached by following the directions given by pollsters. If Moses had responded to opinion polls, he most certainly would not have crossed the Red Sea.

*

No pervert has ever been more articulate than the Marquis de Sade. By recording his sadistic fantasies he has obtained the deserved accolade of having his name perpetuated in every European language. The French analysts, unsurprisingly, have often turned to their fellow countryman to assist them in their divinations of the precipitates of the symptoms presented to them by their pervert patients; for Sade's Code of Laws, in his *120 Days*, sets out with astonishing clarity the rules that must govern the life of a true pervert. Those rules, and the resultant exegesis made by the French analysts, help us to understand the significance of the widespread renaming of Blair. There are more than vestigial traces of Sade's doctrine in 'Tony Blur's' policy presentations.

It must be remembered that Sade's singular imaginative achievement was his creation of a fantasy world where all differences were annihilated; in his perverse universe any notion of organisation, structure or division was suppressed. The goal of the Sadeian hero is the attainment of a complete merging; he is man violently assaulting Nature, eradicating the essence of things and thus instituting what he describes as the 'absolute mixture'. Always, in playing on his constant theme of sexual intercourse, the protagonists he depicts are engaged in group sex, men and women, children and old people, virgins and whores, nuns and bawds, mothers and sons, uncles and nephews, noblemen and rabble: 'All will be higgledy-piggledy, all will wallow, on the flagstones, on the earth, and, like animals, will interchange, will mix, will commit incest, adultery and sodomy.'

In Sade's world all the barriers which separate man from woman, child from adult, mother from son, daughter from father, brother from sister, are broken down; and in elaborate permutation of erogenous zones, all of them are made interchangeable. 'Mixture,' Chasseguet-Smirgel has written, 'would be considered the heading under which the whole of Sade's fantasy world is played.' And to obtain that mixture he conjures up a vision of a devouring digestive tract, an enormous grinding-machine, where all that is taboo, forbidden or sacred is disintegrated and reduced to excrement. The world of differences would be wiped out and in its place would be a world reduced to faeces.

Sade's literary capacity as a pornographer may be unique; but the perversions he describes tease out responses in the thousands who continue to read him, for possession of perverse elements within the psyche is the common lot of mankind. When those elements play a considerable rôle in the cast of mind of a politician, then his outpourings can often deserve to be dismissed as 'mush'; there is not an immeasurable distance between Sade's faecal mixtures and Blair's 'Blurrism'. When *The Times*'s editorials, as in April 1996, state that the charge of Blurrism against Labour sticks, that is a statement of fact; and their complaints that as the outlines of Labour's less contentious policies sharpen, the gaps in the main policy declarations stand out more glaringly, is incontestable. But they err in attributing this solely to a desire on Blair's part to keep his party in the dark and so avoid internal dissension. That policies are so diffused, so lacking in definition, is because such a presentation is endemic to Blair's temperament; a distinctive detailed display of his political wares, each separately to be viewed, is at all costs to be avoided.

'Bubble 'n' Squeak' was therefore an apt heading to be given by Roy Hattersley in his review of *The Blair Revolution*, cowritten by Blair's principal aide. As a political sophisticate with ministerial experience, Hattersley impatiently rejects the mushy *mélange* proffered to him by Peter Mandelson. He vigorously condemns a work he regards as 'banal', 'pretentious' and, above all, 'confused', 'reducing ideas to vague generalities' with passages of 'pure gibberish. The Blair Revolution – wanting Labour to be a "synthesis" which unites the Left and Centre – rejects ideology and replaces it with banalities.' Hattersley's gibes are well deserved, for Mandelson's idealisation of Blair's penchant for 'synthesis' is analogous to Sade's idealisation of his doctrine of faecal 'mixtures'. Sade's eulogies to the fudges he fantasises took him to a lunatic asylum. Blair's fudging, however, may be taking him to the premiership. His blurring is persistent; *The Times*'s editorial of February 1996, mocking his enthusiasm for the lead singer of the rock group Blur, accurately commented: 'His much publicised wooing of Damon Albarn has already won him the nickname "Blur" a hard prod at his soft focus vision.' That 'soft focus vision' led him to make formulations which have become so indistinguishable from Tory policies that by May 1996 he could, in an *Observer* interview, offer 'moderate' Tory MPs a safe haven, promising them legislation and policies which they would be able to support.

What, then, are the ultimate sources of this extraordinary Sade-like desire to deny differences which finds expression in Blair's fudging? Only the naïve would be content to explain it away as mere political tactics, that Blair is just a skilled player of the usual game of equivocating politicians. His political history and its persistence deny such an interpretation. An elucidation of the motivation of those who have such a compulsion to smudge tells us, yet again, of the perverse components that are so embedded in Blair's political outlook. It is Freud's 75-year-old essay *Fetishism* that gives us the clue we require to understand why a compulsive need can arise to deny or belittle differences. Freud explains that the fetishist never, when a little boy, came to terms with his frightening discovery that a significant anatomical difference exists between the sexes; a fetish assists him, for 'the normal prototype of the fetish is a man's penis', and holding on to his fetish enables him to engage in his sexual proclivities while still maintaining the illusion which at one stage of our early development is, Freud tells us, common to all men, that the mother is like the son, that she has a penis. Initially, little boys, horrified at the sight of a woman's genitalia, deny what their eyes are telling them for they interpret it as an intimation of the retaliatory castration by the father that could await them if they acted on their Oedipal desires. For most, the Oedipal phase is worked through and the reality of the differences is reluctantly accepted, but the pervert has carried his initial horror into adulthood. Some indeed, as the casework material presented by psychoanalysts reveals, persist in denial by having fantasies about a phallic mother or, more usually, fantasies where blurring and merging themes predominate as they attempt to deny the uniqueness of each sex and to pretend that men and women are one. None of us, however, escapes unscathed from that early frightening experience, and perverse components can often be observed at work when we see some adults forever recoiling from the unequivocal, always attempting to build bridges over the unbridgeable.

When the infant has sight of and becomes aware of his penisless mother, we see at their most exotic the vain attempts to deny differences; but the child analysts point out that even before the baby is shocked by his discovery, he has already had premonitory experiences which have caused him to struggle against acknowledgements of separateness. From the beginning the suckling babe experiences anxiety when the breast disappears, and the analysts postulate that in order to create internal harmony and psychic peace, he therefore continuously fantasises about the constant presence of the breast and thus, blurring and merging the bodily boundaries between mother and child, he psychically avoids the pain of separation.

More, a little later, the toddler enters a psychosexual stage when, despite the pleasure he experiences because of the stimulation of the rectal nerves when he expels his faeces, defecations are nevertheless accompanied by considerable anxiety; for he fears that the production of faeces represents a dismemberment or loss of body parts. In order to avoid that anxiety, he seeks to annul the experience of loss by retaining faecal products in his rectum; thus, by clinging to his faeces, he makes his bid to avoid separation and so forestall the coming into existence of the dreaded unacceptable difference between himself and the faecal stool.

No one chooses to become a pervert and no one chooses to retain perverse components in his character structure. Our choice is determined for us in our mother's arms; the mother who is able to give a babe a profound sense of security leaves him equipped to face reality and gradually to acknowledge without fear that a separateness exists between him and the mother. Similarly, the mother who encourages the infant on the pot, praising his productive efforts, diminishes his fear of bodily loss and enables him to have the courage to distinguish between his creative faecal products and his own body.

When the babe is a little older and with horror discovers his mother has no penis, it is not inevitable that the child will later become an equivocating adult, taking refuge within a notable and protective mindset shielding him from any recall of the primal revelation of distinction. Whether that occurs or not is largely dependent on the structure of the family system within which the infant finds the Oedipal drama being enacted. The Oedipal wish to possess the mother and supplant the rival father is an impossible wish which, in some way, we must relinquish. The incestuous choice must be forfeited, for if pursued we fear a terrible retaliation. Every boy has to pass through this Oedipal phase when he concentrates sexual wishes upon his mother and develops hostile wishes against his rival father; but how he lives through and later emerges from this traumatic and conflict-ridden phase, a time when the aspiration of the child crumbles under the impact of retaliatory castration fears, depends on the response of the parents.

If the parents respond positively to the primary affectionate and competitive assertiveness of the child, then the Oedipal phase need not be wholly dominated by unassimilated lust and hostility and all the accompanying fears such emotions bring. But if the child has a mother dutiful but too narcissistic to relate sufficiently positively to allay the child's anxieties, and if, too, she is a submissive wife in a household ruled by a domineering unempathic father, then inevitably the sight of a mother without a penis has an unmitigated and more powerful and lasting effect.

The provocations of the feared father stir up the child's hostility; and the stronger that hostility is, the greater is the fear that in retaliation he will be castrated, that he will lose his penis, as he imagines has been the fate of his mother. The potential pervert cannot tolerate the visible depiction of the fate he fears and still, as an adult, denies in his practices and with his fetishes the anatomical differences between the sexes. He is an exceptional product of his early environment, but any child brought up in a household with a similar scenario, as Blair was, is vulnerable and, although avoiding the true pervert's fate, may carry into adulthood embedded in his personality perverse components expressed in a marked distaste for differentiation and a strong preference for the ill-defined. Definition is too evocative of the horrors and fears occasioned by his primal discovery.

The appeal of androgyny, lacking any explicit distinctive male and female genital quality, is, of course, that it cloaks that original discovery; the penis and vagina are covered over and the pain of making a distinction is therefore dodged. Such evasions can find a political expression. The masking of political decisions by an androgynous leader should therefore be seen for what it is, not as a temporary political stratagem but as a psychopathic phenomenon that will not cease when the immediate political tactic has served its purpose.

An androgynous Opposition leader, propelled by his temperament, can successfully proffer a blurred consensus manifesto to a colluding electorate wanting change but no pain. But neither the leader's temperament nor the problems to be overcome will disappear when, with Tony Blair as prime minister, vague aspirations will lead the converted into defined policies. The incoming members of the Labour government will thus speedily find that, adding to the legacy of problems bequeathed to them by 17 years of Tory misrule, are the psychological problems of the Right Honourable Tony Blair.

A Dire Misfit

The economist Will Hutton, now editor of the *Observer*, in his audacious best-seller *The State We're In*, came to the irrefutable conclusion that without drastic change the prospect for Britain is indeed baleful: 'No state in the 20th century has ever been able to recast its economy, political structures and society to the extent that Britain must do, without suffering defeat in war, economic collapse or revolution. Only traumatic events on that scale de-legitimise the existing order to such an extent that a country concedes the case for dramatic change.'

But it is certain that no catalytic event on the scale of defeat in war or total economic collapse is likely to occur. No less certain is that the needed changes eloquently categorised by Hutton will meet fierce opposition; none will be conceded voluntarily. Only a government with courage and will will be capable of ending the protection afforded to vested interests by the Tory hegemony now governing Britain.

Without such government Britain's decline will continue; unemployment of 2–3 million, bearing particularly hard on men, will remain acceptable and millions more will continue to be marginalised, prematurely retired, living off inadequate savings or sick benefit. All these will continue to belong to the bottom 30 per cent of our population that is today effectively socially and economically excluded. Another 30 per cent who are in work that is structurally insecure will continue to be fearful of threats that new forms of casualised, temporary and contract forms of employment are bringing; and increasingly apprehensive that their homes will be a statistic to add to the 300,000 houses that have been repossessed over the last five years. Even the 40 per cent who can count themselves as holding tenured jobs which allow them to regard their income prospects with some certainty know that they are increasingly at risk as their numbers shrink, as they have shrunk over the last decade. Exhortation and pussy-footing will certainly not bring about the radical economic changes that are needed to end the widespread hardships or serious financial anxieties which are presently afflicting the majority of our population.

Unfortunately, under Blair's leadership, only one major proposal – and it is a crass one – to clear away the silt that clogs Britain's economic governance has so far been made; he has willingly participated in a *folie à deux* with Gordon Brown, giving his assent to a pledge by the shadow Chancellor that Labour will create a super-finance ministry and the Treasury, while remaining 'guardian of the nation's finance', will also be a 'ministry for the real economy' with the achievement of a higher rate of growth, lower unemployment and less inequality written into its brief. The Treasury is to be responsible for sound finance *and* for higher economic growth; such a fanciful remit chimes in with Blair's temperament, for he, as ever, wishes to believe the wolf can dwell with the lamb.

By such administrative legerdemain he conjures up the vision where no longer will departments conflict with the Treasury to protect legitimate sectional interests; a benevolent new Treasury will work with them for the same ends and, overnight, the defeatist monetarist Treasury, which for at least 20 years has almost always been wrong and has ruthlessly purged anyone not a True Believer in the basic doctrine of monetarist economics, will be converted into a dynamic super-ministry committed to 'long term economic and social renewal.'

The proposal is a nonsense. The culture of the Treasury was spelled out by Nigel Lawson when he was Chancellor: 'It is the conquest of inflation, and not the pursuit of growth and employment which is or should be the objective of macro-economic policy.' That culture still prevails and, as Anatole Kaletsky has pointed out: 'Even a wholesale change of personnel at the top would not be enough to change the institutional culture.' If the proposal was implemented some of Blair's immediate emotional needs would indeed be met, but it could have one certain result: the Treasury would possess unlimited and dangerous power over the destiny of a future Labour government.

Such an envisaged Treasury – and indeed any Treasury unless brought to heel – would never sanction radical changes to overcome our social problems and in particular the growth and fear of crime within our society, an issue that will play so substantial a part in the coming general election. It is the issue which Blair has handled to his considerable political advantage when, as shadow Home Secretary, he encapsulated his approach in a notable sound-bite 'tough on crime, tough on the causes of crime', a comment which straddles both the populist clamour for punishment and the desires of the informed reformists anxious to direct attention to the aetiology of criminal behaviour.

But the consensus slogan, although seductive, is flawed. 'Tough' yields to the anger and frustration felt by a community threatened by an antisocial minority but reinforces the illusion that harsh punishment will bring us greater social peace and distracts attention from genuine exploration of the roots of crime; there is no seamless compatibility between advocating both harsh punishments and a focus on the causes of violent crime. Indeed, although greeted with understandable incredulity on the part of those whose bitter experiences of the criminal is limited to being victims of crime, the fact is that punishment is often a lure, not a deterrent, for a considerable section of the criminal caste; and when one explores this bizarre phenomenon, a lead is given directing us to the source of so much delinquent behaviour among the young.

During the last debates in the Commons on the abolition of capital punishment, it fell to me after Sidney Silverman, the renowned abolitionist had died, to steer the House to an acceptance of the proposition that the temporary suspension of state strangulation should be made final; and during those debates I repeatedly drew attention to the phenomenon of criminals who had become criminals through a sense of guilt engendered in their childhood. I had found that among the murderers whom I had defended there were those who positively resented my efforts to save them from the gallows; they had killed to die, and indeed more than one-third of murderers, when hanging was in place, pre-empted the court's judgement and killed themselves.

These murderers seeking their death sentences were exhibiting the same syndrome that was often presented to me by criminals facing lesser charges who, if I obtained their acquittal, were resentful but, if convicted and given long sentences, would write me long letters of thanks praising my spirited efforts to defend them and never reproaching me for my lack of success.

In those days, as a young solicitor, the accused pariahs of the city of my birth thronged my waiting-room. I would note how soon after the arrest of one of these habitual criminals, his stance and physical appearance improved. His furtive, hangdog look would seem for a while to slough off him. He was no longer as lost as before; he had indeed been found by courteous police, then less brusque than today, had been questioned by the attentive probation officer and he had acquired a solicitor who displayed interest in him. He was somebody. And, when the great day of the trial came, he stood in the very centre of the stage in the elevated dock. Here the stipendiary magistrate, the prosecuting solicitor, the clerk, the evidential rules and indeed the whole process, as well as his own advocate, protected and respected him. In many courts he was addressed as 'Mr' and when he gave his wild fanciful account denying his guilt, his absurd and improbable story was treated with total seriousness. Until sentence was pronounced, for a little hiatus, he was a person. Then, thrust back into prison, he lapsed once more into his bewildering anonymity – his name taken from him, a number substituted, garbed impersonally, a nobody, utterly confirmed in his lack of identity.

Yet few of these men really wanted to be acquitted. On the contrary, when I succeeded in persuading the court that the case was not proved beyond reasonable doubt, the client would at most mutter a surly and ungracious thank-you. These were the ones who were neurotically burdened with a sense of guilt for the childhood crimes they had committed only in fantasy, who stagger inexorably, like doomed characters in a Greek tragedy, towards the punishments which they demand as their right. Lacking the imagination of a Lawrence of Arabia to justify the flagellations for which they ached and which alone could bring temporary relief, they commit the most petty and stupid of crimes to ensure that the blows of society would fall upon them. To guarantee that their claim for punishment should not be overlooked, some indeed all but leave their visiting-cards behind when they commit their offences. And not infrequently some immediately rush off to the police to enjoy the agony of confession, a few even selecting and insisting on seeing a particular officer in whose presence their self-abasement must be conducted. A very large number, on being challenged, readily offer an incriminating statement which they sign and later repudiate, often suggesting that they have been threatened or beaten into submission by the police. The hapless and embarrassed policeman has in fact only exceptionally yielded in this way to their masochism and in the witness-box tries to step out of the fantasy rôle which his determined victim, with exquisite delight, projects upon him. The charade is maintained until the very end of the trial and the plea of Not Guilty is insisted upon even after conviction; for this is the only way in which the last remnant of self-respect can be maintained. But the defending solicitor who cheats the accused out of his punishment is not loved. It is true that the accused requires someone to present the denial of his guilt with fervour, so that the shameful need for punishment can remain private, but the most terrible denouement is to be acquitted. Fortunately for him, the whole process of a trial in Britain is so constructed that the sadism of the court and the masochism of the accused, though most amply assuaged, are most decently concealed.

Of course, only a minority of offenders – although a more significant minority than is usually conceded – can confidently be said to be criminals through a sense of guilt; but it is one of the sources of criminal behaviour that particularly mocks the ill-informed view that punishment must necessarily act as a deterrent, and it does direct our attention to the unresolved childhood problems that play so significant a part in adult criminal behaviour.

It is a syndrome, however, that certainly does not stand alone as a warning to those who declare themselves to be 'tough on crime'. Infuriating as it may be to those who believe in longer and longer sentences, it is a fact, well established clinically, that for some criminals harsh penalties are a provocation. I have often encountered criminals whose responses have made it clear to me that the essential dynamic behind their criminal behaviour was defiance, with the excitement of breaking the prohibition against burgling a house or sexually assaulting a woman being far more important for them than the actual gaining of stolen goods or experiencing the tumescence accompanying their assault. Mervin Glasser, writing of sexual crimes, tells us:

> Careful exploration of the dynamics of the offence will reveal that the pleasure comes as much, if not more, from the excitement of defying the prohibition as from the sexual acts themselves. Criminals know this 'dicing-with-death' thrill very well, even having a term for it, namely the 'adrenalin factor'.

One of the many problems that society therefore has to face in dealing with criminals is that some of them gain their kicks from the knowledge that their deeds are forbidden; for such criminals, the more their deviant behaviour is universally and intensely forbidden, the more attractive is the offence. Since objective scrutinies reveal that punishment can sometimes provoke and attract crime, we are entitled to question the motivation of those who, irrespective of the evidence, remain so possessed by a drive to punish.

All the many Commons debates on penal issues in which I participated, and all the years I spent, often fruitlessly, as a member of the Home Office Advisory Committee on the Penal System, taught me how difficult it is to gain acceptance of the truism that our failure to handle crime arises from our failure to handle ourselves. As Freud put it so tartly, the law does not forbid that which man is not prone to do. Therefore, 'Thou shalt not kill' or 'Thou shalt not covet thy neighbour's wife' are not merely abstract dicta, general, spontaneously invented prohibitions against the deeds of some few unknown and, as yet, undiscovered evil men. On the contrary, these are commandments issued for the 'average' man with the 'average' propensity. 'Cain,' the American psychiatrist Gregory Zilboorg once commented, 'was not a unique perverted deviation of manhood, and Abraham was not a unique, evil father who in order to flatter the Lord was ready to butcher his son. In other words, the average man is the carrier of the very impulses which are called criminal when they are acted out.'

The anxiety, often although not always disproportionate, that crime causes can spring from our capacity to identify with the criminal's impulse and our fear that we may be tempted to give vent to those impulses within us which are usually inhibited. For millions the temptation can be dampened by reading detective stories and viewing televised murder mysteries; but the anxieties of some, like Home Secretary Michael Howard, can be quieted down only in sudden unconscious denial of any similarity with the criminal when they would hurl themselves upon that criminal with all the power of their aggressive, punitive, destructive hostility.

Michael Howard I always found to be a ninny; the first time I sought to engage him in conversation when we were leaving a committee together he behaved like a frightened rabbit caught in the headlights and he literally then, and subsequently, scarpered away from me the moment it seemed we would encounter each other. To his growing reputation as the worst Home Secretary this century, I would add my assessment that he is the most unmanly of ministers I've ever known. His desperate overdetermined macho display is one of the symptoms of his incapacity to come to terms with his own unconscious aggressivity, which he hurls upon miscreants even as the Mrs Grundys of this world lament and condemn the sexual peccadilloes of those they envy.

What is humiliating to those of us belonging to Old Labour is the sight of New Labour's me-too-ism. Howard's April 1996 White Paper casting aside the accumulated evidence that prison should, in the interests of our society, be used as a last resort and that crime is closely related to social deprivation, has been substantially left unchallenged by Her Majesty's Opposition. It is painfully ironic that it was left to the Lord Chief Justice and his fellow judges to declare that Howard's White Paper's proposals constitute 'a perversion of justice', a condemnation using language accurately describing the nature of those proposals.

But no such unequivocal condemnation has come from Labour's front bench. How could it? Fearful that a frontal attack of the proposals would subvert the leader's affirmation that he is 'tough on crime', his satrap shadow Home Secretary is dumb and only the judiciary has sought to stem the tide of populism which in all penal issues can be roused. It is easier to go with the tide, and a leader who, as has been repeatedly stressed in this book, is so troubled in coming to terms with his own aggression is far more comfortable in joining the chorus of condemnation of the antisocial delinquent than in daring to focus on the epicentre of the eruption of criminal violence which we are witnessing; and that epicentre, whether one surveys the desolate inner city areas teeming with unemployed youth or the drug scene of the children of dual-earning parents, is within our crumbling, stress-ridden family system.

If there is a diffidence in probing the disorders to be found there, it is because such an exploration, as a preliminary to salutary response, means that we often consequently have to confront our own disorders; and that is discomforting. It is so much easier to deny our own disarray and then vengefully to lament the visible and dangerous expression of their turbulence in others.

Once I came so dangerously near to that epicentre of crime that I could not escape without being scorched. I insisted, as a member of the Home Office Advisory Committee on the Penal System, that the issue of conjugal visits for very long-term prisoners should be considered. I assumed that those prisoners were suffering the same sense of deprivation as so many of us did in wartime when serving overseas on isolated postings in desert or jungle; but as I moved through our maximum-security prisons discussing the issue with the possible beneficiaries I found the suggestion strangely causing as much consternation to them as it did to the Home Office officials. The men I was meeting were, for the most part, professional criminals, thoroughly committed to a life of crime, who had mixed freely among the criminal underworld, and most of them were physically tough and vigorous and under 35 years of age; they had committed homicide or near-homicide in pursuance of robbery and were violent and ruthless. Many of their crimes were ambitious and daring; jewel thefts and massive wage snatches were part of their way of life. Yet these desperadoes, including some of the train robbers, beneath their bravado quivered like jellies when one discussed with them the possibility of conjugal visits.

It is not easy to discuss sex, within a prison environment, with an inmate. Apart from the obvious difficulty that the prisoner speedily discerns the sexual viewpoint of the enquirer, and so gives distorted but acceptable replies, there is also the danger that genuine confidences in this domain can become a sort of sexual complicity between the subject and the investigator. The complicity can be experienced as embarrassment or pleasure and, in either event, the confidences may bear little relation to reality. The investigation, insensitively conducted, can indeed falsify its objective and I fear that initially, unaware of what dangerous ground I trod, I proceeded most clumsily.

I was therefore taken aback to find that most of these men proffered to me all the arguments against conjugal visits that I had heard less skilfully assembled by their gaolers. All the practical difficulties of arranging conjugal visits in conditions that combined security with decency were elaborated upon to me by these prim thugs; and they were certainly not slow to damp down my liberal reforming zeal by pointing out the consequences of many fatherless children likely to be born. A tension I sensed when the matter was broached, and their eagerness to shift the conversation to other minor grievances, when seen as a recurring pattern, put me on guard and eventually gave me more insight into their problem.

I was, in fact, cheating and they did not like it. The rules of the game were well understood by them and the prison authorities and I was not observing well-established regulations. A conspiracy existed between gaoler and gaoled; the prisoner was reduced to his desired level of a pre-pubertal child and, in return, he received tranquillity. The pretence that it was his confinement, not his fear, that prevented an adult sexual attitude was under no circumstances to be commented on; while, in the maximum-security blocks, their walls covered with pin-ups, these gangsters swaggered and boasted of their past criminality, they had the excuse that only the prison walls prevented them from being great lovers. The truth was otherwise; the overwhelming majority of them had had no regular relationship with any woman at the time of their arrest.

In the prisons they were back in childhood; even as, when infants, the father was the law imposing his will upon them, so now as an adult, on the occasion of his transgression, he was subject to an all-powerful authority. And they were accepting their quiescent sexuality with relief, for these were flawed men. All of us must, after puberty, break through parental authority to become sexually mature; but to achieve such adulthood means a successful revolt against the father. But we rebel successfully only if we can do this without excessive fear; and these were men who feared freedom.

They yearned to shelter behind an authority, behind the prison's walls, renouncing their maleness in return for protection even as they had, out of terror, subjected themselves to parental authority. For all these killers and brutes came from rejecting, disordered and deprived homes and these miserable men had received no love to temper the fear that we all must overcome to replace our own fathers. It is not surprising that the talk of conjugal relations disturbed them; they knew it was not sex of which we spoke, but of the constrained freedom of adulthood limited by obligations of family, friends, work and society, and this was the type of freedom which frightened them out of their wits. Onanism was their preferred choice; they wanted to be left to their childish sexual activities.

Almost all these damaged men were the products of a brutalised childhood, cursed with violent fathers or a series of intimidating surrogates who from time to time lived with their unmarried or deserted mothers. And as long as the incidence of such precarious family units increases, so, despite all the growth in the number and length of custodial sentences, will the number of criminals abroad multiply in our society. We can fill our stinking gaols so, as now, they contain more prisoners than ever before in our history and we can acquiesce in Howard's plan to build at a cost of billions a score more gaols, but unless we address ourselves to the abject failure and incapacity of hundreds of thousands of frail family units to socialise their children into law-abiding citizens, we shall end beleaguered, as in many parts of the United States, in our own homes.

Thousands of children from low-income and single-parent homes are presently being expelled, because of their uncontrollable violence, from schools in the deprived urban areas; they are being left to roam the streets to begin their careers in crime. To respond to these kids' dilemmas and all the havoc they create in their neighbourhoods with 'lock them up', 'curfew' and 'tough on crime' slogans is sheer self-indulgence; they will as adults return in kind the hostility we direct at them.

But it is not only the children of the poor who are vulnerable and who in turn will make us vulnerable; the equation is not necessarily a simple one between poverty and crime. The children within the dual-income family are often as much at risk and as emotionally abandoned as the truants on the streets of the inner cities. Home-making and child-rearing are more important than designing computer software or marketing box files, and a country that wants to feel safe needs to re-evaluate the worth of unpaid domestic work, whether done by women or men, and then be prepared to pay the cost that such a recasting of our societal values would entail.

But such a recasting, like the reshaping of the economy, requires a defiant government prepared, as was the Labour government of 1945–51, to challenge all the inimical vested interests sheltering under the Tory hegemony. Those of us left who were brought up in the 1930s in distressed areas like South Wales know how profound were the changes in the quality of life that came about for millions as a result of the legislation of the first post-war government; and now, when comparable drastic changes are required, we should recall that those changes were not achieved by accommodation. Even the most benign of changes, like those heralded by the National Health Service Act, were opposed in the Commons by the Tories, who echoed the initial and almost unanimous opposition of the medical profession. No quarter was given or received as post-war Labour created the welfare state and put heavy industry and the utilities under public control.

No such assaults can be expected from Blair. His approach to the problems of crime is in many ways a litmus test; no issue more clearly illustrates the legitimacy of the *Observer*'s editorial criticism of 2 June 1996:

> New Labour has swerved so sharply to the right that it is
> in danger of crashing through the central reservation.
> The presentational spin is that policy should be tough
> and hard choices made; but the direction of the
> toughness seems always to involve a concession to the
> right.

At the least, a genuine response to the growth of crime would
require massive investment in the inner cities, augmentation and
considerable funding of all our family support services,
including adolescent units staffed by child analysts and
psychologists, far more teachers appropriately trained in the
laggard overstretched schools in problem areas, social workers
who have received far more rigorous training than at present,
screening and shaping of those working in our children's homes,
costly retraining of prison officers so that they could become
rehabilitation carers and not turnkeys, and a recognition that a
parent should, by subsidy and tax relief, be enabled to remain at
home during the child's early years.

These or similar preventive responses will not be achieved
by a party of consensus. Such programmes have to be paid for
and that means a redistribution of wealth, a readiness to strip the
City of its fiscal and other privileges, and a frank
acknowledgement that financial sacrifices will have to be made
by those well able to bear them. It means the breaking-up, not
the creation and sustaining, of a governing consensus that is
breeding our present ills, and excites the growth of violent
crime. It means a programme which by temperament rather than
by ideology Blair is inhibited from enacting.

A Rum Entourage

Competitiveness in the House of Commons has always been extraordinarily intense; but now, with the growing professionalisation of British politics, rivalries between those seeking advancement and acknowledgement have flared up as never before. The capacity to suppress the hostile wishes felt against each other by contenders as they work together to obtain or retain power for their party is diminishing; each Member, no longer regarding his political activities as only a part of his life, invests all his narcissism in his personal political success. For too many MPs all their self-worth is measured only by the acclamations and the notice their febrile political activities bring.

The phenomenon of such rivalries is not new; its present vehemence is. As the Conservative Party, effectively leaderless, falls apart, as Portillo, Clarke, Redwood, Howard and Heseltine flay each other, the proffered excuse that they are merely presenting different emphases on policies becomes increasingly unpersuasive. The Conservatives have displayed internecine savagery in the past, as in Macmillan's Night of the Long Knives, but now the hostilities are fought out in open daylight.

Their attacks on one another cease to be encoded and become overt. The Tories, who in the past so often could mask their intra-party hostilities, are now engaged in public brawls; they no longer are able to persuade the public that intra-party hostilities are a monopoly of a loutish Labour Party.

The psychological truth is that in Parliament, in all parties, there operate compulsive drives which prompt these oscillations between brotherhood and fratricide. The behaviour of the present cabinet is occasioned in large measure by the selfsame mechanism that we see operating at the end of Labour Party conferences when men band together, holding hands, singing 'Auld Lang Syne', after they have for days been savaging each other to their political depths. And it is a mechanism which has a particular current relevance when in May 1996, despite the subsequent protestations and denials from Blair, we are accurately informed in the *Guardian* by the perceptive Julia Langdon that: 'The Shadow Cabinet corridor today is not a place suffused with an atmosphere of brotherly love nor with a sense of unity and purpose at the exciting expectation of the prospect of real power. There is, however, jealousy and suspicion and paranoia in plenty ...'

To understand such intense rivalries like those prevailing within Blair's entourage, one needs to note Edward Glover's emphases that early sibling rivalry, giving rise to intense unconscious hostility, can later lead to a positive homosexual attachment to brother-substitutes. Early childhood impulses of jealousy derived from competition against rivals, usually with older brothers for a mother's love, lead to hostile and aggressive attitudes towards those brothers which can reach the pitch of actual death wishes; but these dangerous impulses cannot maintain themselves. Under the influence of upbringing, with the awareness of his continued powerlessness, the little boy's impulses yield to repression and undergo a transformation, so that the rivalries of the earlier period become the first homosexual love object. The process, as Freud has explained, is:

a complete contrast to the development of persecutory paranoia, in which the person who has before been loved becomes the hated persecutor, whereas here the hated rivals are transformed into love objects. It represents too an exaggeration of the process which, according to my view, leads to the birth of social instincts in the individual. In both processes there is first the presence of jealous and hostile influences which cannot achieve satisfaction; and both the affectionate and social feelings of identification arise as reactive formations against the repressive aggressive impulses.

From time to time, however, and at no time more than in the present House of Commons, the repressed aggressive impulses of which Freud writes become so violent that the feelings of identification created with other members of the same party are not powerful enough to contain them. Living as I did for decades in a House plagued always with intrigue and rumour, I was ever aware of the homosexual rivalries that expressed themselves not in overt homosexual conduct but in rationalisations of political policy. These homosexual elements can be distastefully observed as the old Tory loyalties to the party and to each other collapse and, under cover of differing views on ERM or the beef boycott, battles ensue between rival contenders.

In a club like the Commons, male bonding has always played a significant part and within the Conservative Party, with its misogyny and paucity of women members, group identification often holds in check the repressed aggressive wishes. Now the Tory MPs are impaled on their own ideology; mocking 'society', deliberately weakening the group and making an apotheosis of individualism has meant that party ties have slackened and their homosexual rivalries have been able to escape into the public arena. Rivalries of this order are to be clearly distinguished from jealousies that may arise from actual physical sexual relationships; but they are rivalries that can be powerful and destructive.

Among Blair's entourage these rivalries are not even wearing the fig-leaf of ideological or political differences. In May 1996 *The Times*, reporting on the clashes between the two bachelors Gordon Brown and Peter Mandelson, explained:

> Gordon Brown, the Shadow Chancellor, and Peter Mandelson, the Labour leader's long-time adviser, were once the closest of friends. But they have not been on personal speaking terms – other than at formal meetings where contact is unavoidable – for more than 18 months.
>
> Mr Blair is known to be deeply concerned over the failure of two of his truest confidants to be reconciled.

Meantime, to add to this heady brew, the *Guardian*, under the headline 'The bad blood brothers', writes of the tensions between Blair and Brown, and Langdon reports:

> on the fall-out that is shaking the Labour Party ... Gordon Brown has always been the closest political ally of the party leader ... They joined the House of Commons on the same day. They shared an office for years. They shared their dreams and ambitions and their plans, too. It is said that ten years ago, with their friend Peter Mandelson, they sat down and worked out their plan for rebuilding the Labour Party. They were known as the 'twins' and as 'blood brothers'. Their names were once always spoken in the same sentence; Brown and Blair first ... and then order reversed some time in 1992 and they became Blair-and-Brown.

Now it is suggested that the reluctant conceding of Brown to Blair in the contest for the Labour leadership has left its mark:

> For the bitterness remains. The bond between the two men is still there and Brown is still there; at the leader's right hand, at every crucial meeting, on every important platform, one of the four men running the Labour Party, with Peter Mandelson and Alistair Campbell, the insiders say. Tony Blair has an extraordinary friendship with

Brown. He is said to feel beholden to him, to feel guilty that he deprived Brown of the top job.

The stabilisation of this turbulent quartet is unlikely to be assisted by the presence among them of Alistair Campbell, the hyperactive press secretary to Tony Blair. The *Sunday Times*'s 5 May 1996 profile of this character recounts:

> The bagpipe-playing former boozer who began his writing career composing soft porn, and once thumped a journalistic colleague in defence of Robert Maxwell's honour, was last week described by a High Court judge as 'not a witness in whom I could feel 100 per cent confidence'.

And the judge's other admonition, 'less than completely open and frank', adds to the disquiet occasioned by Campbell's CV. After he left Cambridge, where, the *Sunday Times* tells us, he 'specialised in drinking and football', he went in his third year at university to teach in Nice, where he made his debut in soft pornography:

> Then 22, he wrote an article for *Forum* magazine under the headline 'The Riviera Gigolo', recounting the sexual exploits of, well, a Cambridge modern language student teaching in Nice. Other articles followed, one on the pleasures of busking with 'incredibly phallic' bagpipes which turned women on, and another urging sexual athletes to give up smoking; 'the smoker, unfit as he is, is unlikely to be able to keep the bedsprings bouncing all night'.

With such qualifications he went on to work as a journalist on the tabloids, recording how much drink he consumed in a not untypical day: '15 pints of beer, half a bottle of Scotch, 4 bottles of wine with David Mellor at lunch ...' Unsurprisingly, he suffered a nervous breakdown and, to survive, renounced alcohol, resumed his career, worked singularly ambivalently for

Maxwell and was then head-hunted by Blair. Blair thought so much of his talents that he sought him out personally in France on holiday in 1994 to persuade him to take on his present position. He was soon displaying his wiles to his master by masterminding at the 1994 Labour conference the ditching of Clause Four by not distributing in advance the pages of Blair's speech which contained the contentious proposal, and thus opponents were caught off balance.

The excessive warmth and anxieties prevailing among these four men, the permutations in their emotional patterns as they quarrel and reconcile, are of a similar order to those found in the charged hothouse atmosphere of a sixth-form boarding-school where adolescent boys, still wrestling with their sexuality, squabble and make up, forever forming and re-forming cliques as they endeavour to displace their repressed steaming passions on to fault-finding or idealisation of their peers. That not dissimilar immature responses can prevail in a circle governed by a leadership with marked androgynous qualities is predictable.

Robert Harris, an able and discerning writer, senses the combustibility of the situation and tells us: 'A novelist would be hard put to invent a potentially more explosive mixture than that offered by Labour's Big Four.' Homing in on the particular relationship between Blair and Brown, he postulates that these men, once 'close as brothers', now have a relationship possessing a potential for dramatic tension that is almost limitless; and that Brown's unhealed wound 'now runs across the political landscape like a San Andreas fault'.

Harris rightly draws attention to the precedent of the ruptured relationship of Roy Jenkins and Tony Crosland, very close friends for 30 years until, to Crosland's undisguised dismay, Jenkins in 1967 obtained the Chancellorship which Crosland coveted. 'It would be idle to pretend,' wrote Jenkins in his memoirs, 'that these events ... did not leave a scar on Crosland which had the effect of crucially damaging the cohesion of the Labour right over the next eight or nine years.' Harris eloquently concludes, observing the potential for tumult in the

Blair–Brown relationship and the severe political consequences of the Jenkins–Crosland estrangement, that: 'The intangible elusive indefinable action of one human personality upon another is what will make history.'

But Harris's 'intangible' and 'elusive' element, although buried in the unconscious is by no means 'indefinable'. The psychodynamics that Freud delineated most certainly operated in the Jenkins and Crosland quarrel. I had ample opportunity to observe the interplay since, even before I entered the Commons, Crosland, a stimulating guest for me but not for my wife – since he was almost invariably petulant with women – would stay with us at our Welsh home.

It is understandable that when quarrels occur between politicians who have long and deep friendships, and who share a common ideology, the cause of the break is attributed to 'ambition'; but that is too simplistic a diagnosis. All of us, men and women, have homosexual components within our make-up, but how we deal with them, whether as in homophobia we fearfully and vainly endeavour to repudiate their presence, whether we sublimate them in a bonding to advance a political or religious cause, whether we deploy them within a heterosexual relationship to enrich our identification and empathy with our partner, whether they find expression in overt sexual conduct – however they are managed or manage us, what is irrevocable is their continuing presence; they cannot be cancelled out. And Edward Glover, who incited me to end the criminality of adult homosexual conduct, always reminded us that Freud had emphasised that hate constitutes one of the aetiological factors in homosexuality. As Glover expressed it: 'Earlier jealousy and rivalry can be resolved or countered or kept in successful repression by what we might call a reaction formation of homosexual attachment.'

With jealousies and rivalries forever simmering beneath homosexual elements, there are those who, because they find those elements to be too compulsive and untamed to be dealt with by any other means, turn to a 'reaction formation of homosexual attachment' which may or may not take an overt form. It is, however, a reaction formation fraught with hazards, for even if slightly punctured, the jealousies and rivalries beneath burst, often with terrifying force. The disputatious senior common rooms of Oxbridge colleges, as I have noted when invited to their High Tables, are littered with the intellectual debris of exploded homosexual attachments. The syndrome notoriously displayed in those quarrelsome academic circles is no less on show in Blair's inner circle.

There is, therefore, a particular irony that to support him in the election year, Blair has called back to London from Australia his old Oxford mentor Peter Thomson, disciple of Macmurray, who brings 'glad' tidings that are unlikely to dispel the foetid atmosphere of Blair's quartet; for as Thomson explained in June 1996, he brings with him his favourite quote from the Scottish moral philosopher: 'All meaningful action is for the sake of friendship.' 'But I want no rôle,' he explained, now that Blair has found for him the vicarage of St Luke's, Holloway, 'other than friendship.' Doubtless he will find responses to his message at self-styled post-evangelical St Luke's, a happy-clappy, pewless, uncluttered world filled by trendy young Christians much addicted to histrionic audience participation in services that can start with a man dragging a full-sized cross across the floor and then continue in a demotic style of worship which would cause traditional Anglicans to choke on their vespers. But because the message is fatally flawed, far from finding resonances within Blair's circle, it is more likely to excite further rivalry and heighten existing tensions.

It has been seen, when exploring Macmurray's Boy Scout proselytising themes, that his constant affirmations 'that the noblest form of human existence is friendship', and that, in friendship as in community, antagonism and estrangement lead only to 'despair', contain a massive denial of the ambivalences that must pervade any genuine flesh and blood relationship (see pages 96–9); that to seek to outlaw the inherent aggressiveness within sexuality is a vain quest, and can lead only to distortions of the human spirit which can have lamentable personal and social consequences.

For the restless Thomson, the one-time 'mature' theological student, one-time Australian television newsreader, one-time estate agent, twice thrown out of his parishes, one-time headmaster of an Australian public school and one-time farmer, to bring stability to the quartet seems in itself improbable; but, more serious, the doctrine this cove emphasises, far from directing attention to the causes of the inner circle's disharmony, the androgynous and homoerotic elements with which it is excessively infused, would totally deny their existence, and preaching sweetness and light and 'pure' friendship would ensure, since sex and aggression when repudiated will always hit back and wage incessant guerrilla war, that the present discords will swell into a deafening cacophony.

Already it is difficult to parry comments like those in a hostile *Times* editorial of May 1996 where, having remarked that the infighting within the circle is 'surprisingly non-ideological', the writer concluded that 'the fact they are so driven by personal animosities exposes how immature many of Labour's senior politicians are'. If Thomson is to become, under Blair's patronage, a part-time member of a new quintet, a maturational process is certainly not going to be the result.

Some of us have been here before. The seedy kitchen cabinet of Harold Wilson contributed not a little to the less than glorious record of his governments. Wilson's kitchen cabinet both mirrored and provided corroboration of his worst features. Now a nascent kitchen cabinet for the incoming Labour government is coming into existence, not through political chance or political pressures; it is the creation of Tony Blair, with its members attracted to him, and serving and reflecting his emotional needs, and consequently a pretty rum crew they prove to be.

Deadwood

In June 1996 Blair put his name to a contribution in *Prospect*. There, provocatively, in manic mood, speaking of his New Labour Party, he triumphantly announced: 'We have cleared out the deadwood of outdated ideology, policy and organisation.' The referents no doubt included veterans like myself but although, since I am a near octogenarian, he is only a little premature in announcing my own funeral, he fortunately gravely errs in believing that there is no life left for Old Labour.

He is mistaking silence for acquiescence. The loyalties of the traditional core of the Labour Party are being exploited; and Blair is relying on their allegiances not to break ranks, even as he outrageously repudiates all their essential values. He is relying too on their defeatism. The exclusion of the party from government for so many years, the hopes raised and then dashed at the last election, have left them lacking confidence in victory; and well-intentioned counsel, as from Will Hutton, that political alliances must be in place to ensure victory, and concerned reproaches from Robert Harris against Roy Hattersley for presuming publicly to demur from Blair's directives, all help to create a political mood where criticism is quenched lest it helps the Tories to retain power. Meantime Blair, with deliberation, continues to raise what the ever-shrewd observer Ian Aitken has described as the 'anxiety level' within the party by warning dissidents that express criticism means electoral failure.

For me, these apprehensions recall all those existing in 1945 when so many of the political 'sophisticates' on the left, believing it was incredible that Churchill could be dislodged by the Labour Party alone, were urging caution and alliances; indeed, the Communist Party, then a relevant force in British politics, called for a government of National Unity to be created. That timidity was not shared by those of us in the ranks in the Forces, and I still retain yellowing sheaves of articles which I as a young man wrote mocking those who, after the wilderness years of the 1930s, could not believe in the prospect of an overwhelming Labour victory. There are rare moments in British politics when elections can yield far more than a mere alternation of office-holders: 1945 was such a moment, and so is now.

There is a tide in the affairs of men which must be taken at the flood, and 'on such a sea we are now afloat'. We are living under a totally discredited, decrepit and demoralised regime, one that is about to be swept away. The estrangements within the Tory Party are chronic, and no political cosmetics will heal them. Amidst the clamour of Tory self-destruction, there is no need for Old Labour to talk in whispers, although Blair's spin doctors would seek to persuade us otherwise.

Those spin doctors have been trenchantly attacked by Joy Johnson, the Labour Party's former media director, who quit her post rather than endure their antics. She deplores their 'language of exclusivity'; they speak a ghetto language, a tongue which is confined to a small Westminster enclave. There we find 'the lobby feeding off the politicians and the politicians feeding off the lobby – traipsing between Number Four Millbank, the broadcasting centre for BBC, Sky TV and ITN and the House of Commons. Our political post has become a story of sophisticated games with rules only understood by the few.' Old Labour needs neither to unravel those rules nor to abide by them; nor do we need to demean ourselves by using their debased marketing vocabulary.

If Britain is to arrest its decline, if our infrastructure is to be developed and refurbished, if our social education and health services are to be adequately funded, if poverty and homelessness are to be alleviated, then Labour needs to use its traditional language and direct it against its traditional enemies; never was it more relevant than today to assail finance-capitalism. The City and the bankers, in their greed for ever more obscene profits, in their notorious short-termism, are frustrating the development of British technology and sabotaging the growth of manufacturing industries upon whose wealth creation depends the fulfilment of our aspirations to have a happier and more just society.

But the institutions, if permitted, will continue to seek speedy dividends and eschew involvement in, and responsibility for, long-term investment in industries, and the bankers will not easily come out of their anonymous centralised citadels to journey to the smaller manufacturers in the regions. The culture of the takeover bid, of defensive asset-stripping, of the slashing of research funding, will, unless seriously challenged, continue to envelop the Square Mile. And the City walls, protecting the malpractices, are high and thick; they will not fall to Blair's muted trumpets. Strong legislative battering-rams and tough fiscal policies will be needed before those walls crumble. Indeed, if the July 1996 economic forecast of Anatole Kaletsky, so often accurate in his prognostications, is correct, then his recommendation that the response to a coming 1997 consumer boom must be tough fiscal policies means a bold Labour government would have economic as well as equitable justifications to increase taxes on those well able to bear them.

But if the needed confrontational stances, so alien to Blair's temperament and emotional needs, are not taken up by the incoming Labour government, then disillusion will soon follow.

It is wiser now to sound the tocsin and unequivocally to identify the flaws of the man who may be Britain's next prime minister. When he arrives in Downing Street he will have at his disposal the armoury of patronage and a legislature that has, under Thatcher, yielded too much of its leverage to the executive. But no prime minister has absolute power, and the pace and quality of legislation and related government action depend upon his cabinet, the pressures of his back-benchers, and from the activists and local councillors in his party away from Westminster.

Aware of the potential pressures, defensively, Blair and his entourage have devised the scheme of a ballot of all members to approve the party manifesto provisionally set out in July in *The Road to the Manifesto*, and they must approve it as a package; no amendment or addition is to be allowed. More skilful spin doctors would have avoided bestowing such a title, one telling of highways, on the document, for to Old Labour it immediately recalls the famous gibe of Nye Bevan against those who, 40 years ago, sought to move the Labour Party to the centre: 'We know what happens to people who stay in the middle of the road. They get run down.'

But in any event, is this manifesto really of any importance? Few such party manifestos are; but there was one important exception. In 1858, in London, at the request of a handful of émigré political refugees, tailors and print-workers, the 29-year-old Marx and 28-year-old Engels composed *The Communist Manifesto*, that extraordinary compound of the universal and particular which, for good and bad, was over the decades to become the accepted creed for millions of mankind. Marx's document was of similar length to Blair's proposed manifesto. It moved the earth; Blair's manifesto would not cause the slightest tremor in a City bank. But Blair, to trap his party members into irrevocable commitment, would elevate its importance, so that every sentence in the flaccid document should be regarded in future as a sacred text binding Labour Party members who, to retain or gain membership, are now to be called upon to declare themselves as devotees of this insipid holy writ; and meantime, to ensure non-believers within the older membership can be swamped, Blair, in well-advertised recruitment drives, builds up his new personal electorate.

In practice, of course, governance, after elections, is almost always shaped by the exigent, not by the proclaimed priorities within vote-baiting manifestos; as Harold Macmillan told us, the real determinants are 'events, events'. And this manifesto will certainly leave the Labour government open to be determined by events; those events will fill the vacuum within this manifesto. It is a manifesto which will be remembered, if at all, by what it has left out, rather than what it ambiguously promises. It is a manifesto not wordless, but one deficient in verbs, for verbs import action, specific deeds, and these are largely eschewed. The *Guardian*'s Simon Hoggart, far too experienced a political observer to be bemused by Blair, has in penetrating parody described his reaction as he listened to the leader's presentation of *The Road to the Manifesto*:

> As so often in a Blair speech, as it progressed, it began to shed verbs. Sentences were reduced to a cluster. Nouns and pronouns. Sentences, verbless.
>
> 'Fairness at work. Practical proposals. In crime, tough on crime, tough on the causes of crime. In Europe, leadership not isolation ...
>
> 'In every area policy is New Labour.' (Sorry, that does contain a verb, but sounds as if it doesn't.) 'Smaller classes. Shorter waiting lists. A turning point in British politics. New Labour. New Life for Britain.'
>
> For too long, the party's energy wasted. On verbs. For the British people, now, no more verbs. Tough on verbs, tough on the causes of verbs. New Labour. New nouns, adjectives. Real words. Words for a new Britain.
>
> There is a purpose to this. Verbless sentences sound as if they are firm promises. The mind supplies the missing phrases: 'we shall provide ... we will legislate for ...'
>
> Yet nothing concrete has been proposed. Like so much

of the manifesto, each verbless phrase offers a fine aspiration, worthy in every way, utterly estimable, and entirely vague.

But vague as it is, certain directions are only too clear. Barbara Castle, a great fighter, loathing the prevarication and ageism enveloping the document as expressed in its policy U-turn reversing Labour's plan for basic state pensions to rise in line with earnings, has defiantly said that this unalterable manifesto was making the vote upon its contents 'a loyalty test – like an election in a one-party state'. And that is precisely what it is. Blair, blackmailing what Barbara Castle has called a 'supine National Executive', arrogantly replied, when asked whether the whole stratagem of manifesto and ballot is another example of centralising power in his hands: 'With a modern political party you have to have effective ways of decision-making. My attitude has always been: if you don't like the leader, get rid of the leader and get someone else in to do the job.'

As Blair in the summer of 1996 in a series of private meetings wooed Labour MPs in an endeavour to avoid contentiousness in the annual elections to the shadow cabinet, some present played a little game. They counted the number of times Blair in his presentations used the first person singular and how many times the first person plural; 'we' had no score but the 'I's proliferated. With the favourable opinion polls inflaming his narcissism it increasingly emerges, publicly and unmortified. His MP audiences, noting these personality traits and becoming increasingly wary, resisted his blandishments. In the subsequent ballot 80 MPs refused to vote for his Shadow Chancellor and Home Secretary, and to make their resentments no less explicit placed the most prominent woman dissident high in the poll. The *Guardian* editorial pertinently commented: 'These were not the actions of a party marching confidently to victory and the agreed implementations of its programme. They were the actions of a party showing serious strains about important parts of the leader's projections.'

Blair's response to the warning those elections gave was dictated by his emotional needs not those of his party. In the subsequent shadow cabinet reshuffle, he demoted those not prepared to submit unconditionally to his ukase, and let it be known his Whips were to prepare tougher disciplinary measures against those MPs who dared to demur. Consensus, his false consensus, was to be inviolable; plurality could not be tolerated.

His only concession to those resentful of the timidity of his programme was to preach patience, explaining it will take time and continuous Labour governments to bring about the needed changes. This is the counsel of the pusillanimous; it is not patience that is required, but impatience. Any halfwit can work according to the doctrine that politics is the art of the possible; all my legislative experience tells me that politics worth the candle is the art of the impossible.

This is certainly not the time to speak of distant horizons; in politics too they recede as one advances towards them. The defeatism that pervades Whitehall and, in particular the Treasury, should not be allowed to so overwhelm the Labour Party that its goal becomes little more than good management of a Britain deemed to be in inevitable decline; and it is because Blair's consensus politics essentially accommodates itself to that defeatism that Blair treats as relics those within the Labour Party who use their radical socialist traditions to challenge that assumption.

Despite his endeavours Blair has not yet succeeded in firmly pinning the label of anachronism upon British socialism, and, although he has inflicted self-doubt on some within the Labour movement who, to gain government, believe there is no alternative but to accept post-Thatcherite pollution as a permanent feature of our political environment, there is no such inevitability. I have too often seen politicians use that type of historicism as an excuse for inaction and I have always admired Leon Trotsky's scorn of 'the pusillanimity of an historic fatalism which in all questions, whether concrete or private, passively seeks a solution in general laws and leaves out of the count the mainspring of all human decisions – the living and acting individual'. It remains open to us, young and old, who find Blair's imprint upon the Labour Party unacceptable to prove that his dismissal of Old Labour as 'deadwood' is the most colossal arboreal misjudgement in contemporary politics.

If there are those in political life who, sadly, from the start, from their earliest years, through external circumstances, are faulted, then it is not for us to relieve them of their private neurotic traits by condoning their transference to the public domain; that is one step too far in de-privatisation.

The cynical, the over worldly-wise, and the well-intentioned faint-hearted will certainly affirm that whatever may have been the psychodynamic or psychopathology that brought him to his leadership, Blair's hijacking of the Labour Party is complete and irrevocable; and that those engaged in subversion – as is the declared intention of this book – are foolishly nostalgic and out of kilter with the times.

Unfashionable we certainly are; but I am no stranger to that condition, for enduring the opprobrium attached to expounding initially unfashionable minority causes was a precondition to achieving the social reforming legislation with which I am associated, and which in my old age now comforts me for all the years I gave to the House of Commons.

On many occasions during those years, when fighting against the tide, I recalled and drew strength from the insight of Sigmund Freud, who, in rallying his associates facing the scepticism of their patients and the hostility of a puritanical society, would end his letters to them with the motto '*Coraggio*'. Similar courage is now needed by all those understandably hesitating, lest it props up a crumbling discredited government, to express their profound unease with Blair's leadership; but passivity now could mean a future Labour government would be a poor thing, a mere mirror image of a blurred mirror image, the image of the Right Honourable Tony Blair. And so I presume to counsel *Coraggio, Coraggio*.

Bibliography

Aberbach, D, 'Charisma and attachment theory', *International Journal of Analysis*, vol.76, part 4, August 1995

Abraham, K, *Selected Papers on Psychoanalysis*, Hogarth Press, 1954

Abse, D W, *Excellence and Leadership in a Democracy*, ed Stephen R Graubard & Gerald Holtom, Columbia University Press, 1962

Abse, D W, 'Charisma, Anomie and the Psychopathic Personality', address to the first International Congress on Social Psychiatry, August 1964

Abse, D W, *Hysteria* (2nd edn), Wright Bristol, 1987

Abse, L, *Private Member*, Macdonald, 1973

Abse, L, address to International Society for the History of Rhetoric, Oxford, 1985

Adcock, F, *Sunday Times*, 10 December 1995

Aldred, C, *Akhenaten: Pharaoh of Egypt*, Thames & Hudson, 1968

Anderson, B, *The Times*, 28 September 1995

Berlin, I, *Against the Current*, Oxford University Press, 1981

Blair, A C L, 'Let Us Face the Future', Fabian pamphlet 571, Fabian Society

Bowlby, J, *Attachment and Loss*, Hogarth Press, 1973

Breasted, J H, 'Ikhnaton, the Religious Revolutionary', *Cambridge Ancient History*, 1st edn, vol.II, ch.6, Cambridge, 1924

Burden, R, *New Statesman*, 11 August 1995

Byron, G G, *Don Juan*, canto 1

Chasseguet-Smirgel, J, *The Ego Ideal: The Malady of the Ideal*, Free Association Books, 1985

Chasseguet-Smirgel, J, *Creativity and Perversion*, Free Association Books, 1985

Demause, L, *Foundations of Psycho-History*, Creative Roots, 1982

Edmonds, J, *Tribune*, 11 August 1995

Elovitz, P, 'Clinton's Childhood, and First Year in Office', *Journal of Psycho-History*, vol.XXI, no.3, Winter 1994

Fairbairn, W R D, *Psychoanalytical Studies of the Personality*, Routledge & Keegan Paul, 1990

Falk, A, *Herzl King of the Jews*, University Press of America, 1993

Foot, M, *Aneurin Bevan*, Davis-Poynter, 1973

Freud, S, *Leonardo da Vinci*, SE, XI, Hogarth Press

Freud, S, *Totem and Taboo*, SE, XIII, Hogarth Press

Freud, S, *On Narcissism: An Introduction*, SE, XIV, Hogarth Press

Freud, S, *Some Neurotic Mechanisms in Jealousy, Paranoia and Homosexuality*, SE, XVIII, Hogarth Press

Freud, S, *Fetishism*, SE, XX1, Hogarth Press

Frith, S, & Goodwin, A (eds), *On Record: Rock, Pop and the Written Word*, Routledge, 1990

Gallup Poll, *Daily Telegraph*, 7 February 1994

Glasser, M, 'Some Aspects of the Rôle of Aggression in the Perversions', essay in *Sexual Deviation*, ed Ismond Rosen, Oxford University Press, 1979

Glover, E, *Aggression and Sado-Masochism*, in *The Pathology and Treatment of Sexual Deviation*, ed Ismond Rosen, Oxford University Press, 1964

Griffin, R, *The Nature of Fascism*, Routledge, 1993

Guntrip, H, *Schizoid Phenomena, Object-Relations and the Self*, Hogarth Press, 1968

Harris, R, *Sunday Times*, 31 March 1996

Hildebrand, P, *Beyond Mid-Life Crisis*, Sheldon Press, 1995

Hoggart, S, *Guardian*, 5 July 1996

Hutton, W, *The State We're In*, Jonathan Cape, 1995

Hutton, W, 'The 30 30 40 Society', *RSA Journal*, March 1996

Johnson, J, *Tribune*, 31 May 1996

Kaletsky, A, *The Times*, 9 January 1996

Kaletsky, A, *The Times*, 16 May 1996

Kaletsky, A, *The Times*, 11 July 1996

Kohut, Heinz, *The Restoration of the Self*, International Universities Press, 1977

Krohn, A, *Hysteria: The Elusive Neurosis*, International Universities Press, 1978

Laplanche, J, & Pontalis, J B, *The Language of Psychoanalysis*, Hogarth Press, 1973

Laslett, P, *A Fresh Map of Life*, Weidenfeld & Nicolson, 1989

Lawson, Alvin H, 'Placental Catarrhs, Umbilical Mikes and the Maternal Rock-Beat: Verse Fantasies and Rock Music Videos', *Journal of Psycho-History*, vol.XXI, no.3, Winter 1994

Loewenberg, P, 'Theodor Herzl: A Psychoanalytic Study in Charismatic Political Leadership', in *The Psychoanalytic Interpretation of History*, ed Benjamin Wolman, Basic Books, 1971

Macmurray, J, *Persons in Relation*, Faber & Faber, 1961

Macmurray, J, *The Self as Agent*, Faber & Faber, 1961

McSmith, A, *John Smith: A Life 1938–1994*, Mandarin Paperbacks, 1994

Mandelson, P, & Liddle, R, *The Blair Revolution: Can New Labour Deliver?*, Faber & Faber, 1996

Morgan, O, *Keir Hardie*, Weidenfeld & Nicolson, 1975

MORI poll, *The Times*, 31 March 1994

MORI poll, *The Times*, 29 April 1994

Parris, M, *The Times*, 2 June 1995

Plato, *Symposium*, trans. Walter Hamilton, in *The Penguin Book of International Gay Writing*, Viking, 1995

Platt, S, *Guardian*, 29 September 1995

Plumb, J, *The Death of the Past*, Macmillan, 1978

Poirot-Delpech, B, *Le Monde*, April 1995

Pollock, G, 'Ageing or Aged: Development or Pathology', in *The Course of Life*, ed Bethesda, NIMH, 1980

Quine, M S, *Population Politics in 20th-Century Europe*, Routledge, 1996

Raven, C, *Observer*, November 1995

Rentoul, J, *Tony Blair*, Little, Brown, 1995

Reynolds, S, & Press, J, *The Sex Revolts: Gender Rebellion and Rock 'n' Roll*, Serpent's Tail, 1995

Ryecroft, Charles, *A Critical Dictionary of Psychoanalysis*, Yelson, 1968

Selbourne, D, *New Statesman*, 11 August 1995

Simpson, M, *Independent*, 6 March 1996

Skidelsky, R, 'Language and Politics', *Spectator*, 18 June 1977

Smith, D, *Aneurin Bevan and the World of South Wales*, University of Wales Press, 1994

Smith, D, *Sunday Times*, 24 September 1995

Sopel, J, *Tony Blair the Moderniser*, Michael Joseph, 1995

Steiner, G, *In Bluebeard's Castle*, Faber & Faber, 1971

Steiner, R, 'Hermeneutics or Hermes-mess?', in *International Journal of Psychoanalysis*, vol.76, part 3, June 1995

Tait, N, address to the Cambridge Institute of Education, May 1995

Taylor, A J P (ed), *Churchill: Four Faces of the Man*, Penguin, 1973

Townsend, P, *Independent on Sunday*, 14 January 1996

Trilling, L, *Sincerity and Authenticity*, Oxford University Press, 1974

Weber, M, 'Law in Economy and Society', in *Twentieth-*

Century Legal Philosophies Series, vol.VI, M Rheinstein, ed, Harvard University Press, 1954

Weber, M, *The Theory of Social and Economic Organisation*, chap.3, translated by A M Henderson & T Parsons, Oxford University Press, New York, 1947

Wills, G, *Certain Trumpets*, Simon & Schuster, 1995

Winnicott, D W, *The Maturational Processes and the Facilitating Environment*, H Karnac, 1990

Winnicott, D W, 'Through Paediatrics to Psychoanalysis', H Karnac, 1992

Woolf, Ernest S, *Treating the Self: Elements of Clinical Psychology*, Ilford Press, 1988

Young, H, *Guardian*, 3 October 1995

Zilboorg, G, *The Psychology of the Criminal Act and Punishment*, Hogarth Press, 1955

Index

Aberbach, David, 107
Abraham, Karl, 74–5
Abse, Leo: and *in vitro* research, 7; enters Parliament, 18; on Gaitskell, 18–19; on Wykehamists, 20–21; on Nye Bevan, 29–31; and 'B', 37–8; and Matrimonial and Family Proceedings Bill, 53–7, 58–9, 60, 61; his initial impressions of Tony Blair, 56–7; on theatre and politics, 66–7; on Herbert Morrison, 72–3; on Robert Davies, 90–91; and adoption, 116–8; on Blair and the Idea, 159–60; on crime, 189–92, 194–5, 196–7, 198
Adcock, Fleur, 135–6
'Adrenaline factor', the, 191
Ageing, 161–3
Ageism, 151–4, 160–61, 213

Aggression, 98, 99, 100–101; and perversion, 172–4; and infant life, 174–5, 176; and group identification, 200–201
Aitken, Ian, 209
Akhenaten, Pharaoh, 165–6
Albarn, Damon, 181
Androgyny, 132, 133–4, 135, 142–3, 167; and leadership, 164, 167–85, 207; and politics of perversion, 167–8, 184–5
Aphanisis, 111–12
A Political Kiss, 135

Bauer, Otto, 155, 156
Benn, Tony, 78, 120
Berlin, Isiah, 80–81
Bevan, Aneurin, 11, 18, 19, 21, 22, 25, 46, 85, 144, 163, 211; the orator, 29, 30–31, 32–3, 34–5, 39, 42, 45; aggression of,

31, 34, 42; and rhetoric of
sexual inadequacy, 31–2, 33;
his relationship with his
mother, 33, 34, 38; the constituency MP, 35–6; and Welsh
women voters, 35–6; his hermaphrodite qualities, 36, 40,
46–7, 164; marriage of, 36; and
women, 38–9; and John
Strachey, 39–40; millenarianism
of, 40–41; and use of the Bible,
43; on change, 45–6; capitu-
lation on unilateral nuclear disarmament, 47; on the
politician as actor, 68, 69
Bevan, Margaret May, 36
Bevan, Phoebe, 33
Bevin, Ernest, 144
Bible, The, 43, 109–10
Blair, Anthony Charles Lynton,
see Blair, Tony
Blair, Cherie, 107, 142; childhood
of, 119–20; joins Labour
Party, 120; opportunism of,
120; her insecurity, 123; her
narcissism, 123, 124
Blair, Hazel, 88, 110, 113, 176,
177
Blair, James, 115, 118
Blair, Leo, 64, 79–83, 84, 107,
110, 112–13, 114, 115, 116,
118, 119
Blair Revolution, The, 181
Blair, Tony, 49, 56–7; attitude to
John Smith, 6, 7–8; rootless-
ness of, 7, 111, 115; and 1994
leadership election 9–10; charismatic appeal of, 11, 15–16,
50; and religion, 43, 83, 92, 97,
130; his abhorrence of conflict,

59–60, 61, 63, 65, 98, 127,
155, 172, 176, 187, 211; the
placatory skills of, 65, 128–9,
176; the actor, 68; and use of
language, 68; and stagecraft,
69, 84, 90, 115; exhibitionism
of, 71, 77, 88, 97; father's
influence upon, 79, 80, 81–4;
and alienation, 83, 84–5, 88–9,
109; his education, 83–5,
88–90; and the mechanism of
disavowal, 87, 88, 94; his ideas
of community, 92–3, 94–6, 98,
172; origins of his consensus
politics, 99, 100–101; and
homogamy, 107–8, 121; and
aphanisis, 111–13; and his
father's heritage, 114–16,
118–19; the narcissism of, 123,
124, 150, 213; and rock music,
130–43, 172, 176; his views on
regeneration, 148, 149, 150,
154, 155–6; his attitude to the
elderly 150–51, 152, 153, 159,
160–61, 213; his obsession
with modernisation, 154–5,
162; and perversion, 171,
172–3, 176, 177; his
aggression, 176–7, 179, 193;
his need for psychic stability,
177, 178–9; and 'Blurrism',
180–82, 212; the origins of his
androgynous leadership style,
183–5; on crime, 188–9, 193,
197–8; his inner circle, 202–4,
205–7; and 'deadwood', 208–9,
his autocratic temperament,
213–14
Blair, William, 118
Blum, Léon, 155

Blur, 134, 181
Bonaparte, Napoleon, 80
Booth, Gale, 119, 120
Booth, Lyndsey, 119
Booth, Tony, 119, 120
Bowie, David, 142
Bowlby, John, 106
Braun, Eva, 32
Breasted, James, 165
'Breed', 136
Brittan, Leon, 4
Brown, Gordon, 9, 187, 202, 203, 204
Browning, Robert, 163
Bush, George, 128
Byron, Lord, 97

Callaghan, Audrey, 119
Callaghan, James, 18–19, 61,67, 117
Campaign for Nuclear Dis- armanent, 18
Campbell, Alistair, 202, 203–4
Castle, Barbara, 213
Charisma, 11, 15–18, 24, 25, 32–3, 48, 49, 50; the herma- phrodite leader and, 40, 164–7
Chasseguet-Smirgel, Janine, 170, 171, 180
Cherub Rock, 140–41
Children's Act, The (1975), 118
Child Support Agency, 56
Churchill, Randolph, 108
Churchill, Winston, 108, 110, 122, 123, 125, 209
Cicero, 42–3
Clarke, Kenneth, 199
Clause Four, 65, 85, 204
Clinton, Bill, 126–9
Cobain, Kurt, 137

Communist Manifesto, The, 211
Congressional Union of England and Wales, 147
Consensus, 60–62, 99, 100–101, 102–3, 104
Conservative Party: its father- orientated nature, 31; intra- party hostility in, 200, 201; *see also* Thatcher, Margaret
Cook, Robin, 9
Crime, 188–96; and return to childhood, 195–6
Cripps, Stafford, 78, 125, 144
Crosby, 120
Crosland, Tony, 204–5

David, King, 15
Davies, Robert, 90–91
Da Vinci, Leonardo, 170
'Deadwood', 208–9
De Gaulle, Charles, 48
Demause, Lloyd, 138–9
Denial *see* disavowal
De Sade, Marquis, 170, 179–81, 182
Devolution, 3–5
Disarmament debate, 18, 22, 23, 47
Disavowal, 87, 88, 98
Disraeli, Benjamin, 43, 63, 80
Dissatisfaction, 8–9
Dissolution, fear of, 72–4, 75–6
Divorce Reform Act (1969), 53, 54, 55, 59, 60
Doors, The, 134
Durham, 110–11
Durham Cathedral Choristers' Preparatory School, 83
Durham Conservative Associa- tion, 82

Ebbw Vale, 36, 37
Edmonds, John, 62
Engels, Friedrich, 211
Eternal Youth syndrome, 154
European Commission, The, 151
Exhibitionism, 69–70; and idealisation of the mother, 71–2; and inadequate mothering, 74–5, 76, 88

Fairbairn, W R D, 100
False consensus, 61
Fascism, 148–9, 157
Fetishism, 182–5
Fettes College, 84, 88–9
Financial Times, 133
Foot, Michael, 48, 49–50, 144
Forum, 23
Freud, Sigmund, 56, 72, 99, 114–15, 165, 166, 170, 182, 192, 200, 201, 205, 215; on dissatisfaction, 8–9; on homosexuality, 39; on disavowal, 87; on the death wish, 112; on love objects, 123–4; on hysteria, 155
Frith, Simon, 141
Frölich's syndrome, 165, 166

Gabriel, Peter, 140
Gaitskell, Hugh, 11, 36, 37; and Bevanites, 18, 47; seductive voice and charm of 19–20, 21, 23, 24; his elitist style of leadership, 20, 21, 23, 25, 164; his lack of inner freedom, 22; the passivity of, 22; his passion for dancing and music, 22–3; others' views on, 24, 25; his magic circle, 24; and the 1955 leadership election, 25; and the 1959 general election, 25; the final illness of, 25–6; the revisionism of, 41

Gallup polls, 10
Gambetta Léon Michel, 80
Gandhi, Mahatma, 11, 17, 101
Garibaldi, Giuseppe, 80
Garrick, David, 67
Gladstone, William Ewart, 43
Glassner, Dr Mervin, 171, 172, 175, 191
Glover, Edward, 172, 173, 200, 205
Great Exhibition, The, 161
Griffin, Roger, 146
Griffiths, James, 76
Guardian, 57, 85, 99, 132, 200, 202, 212, 213
Guilt, and punishment, 188–91
Guns 'n' Roses, 134
Guntrip, Harry, 100

Hampstead Group, The, 24
Hardie, Keir, 147–8
Harris, Robert, 179, 204–5, 208
Hattersley, Roy, 181, 208
'Heart-shaped Box', 137
Hendrix, Jimi, 139
Hermaphrodite qualities, 40, 50, 166, 167; and Bevan, 46–7, 164; and leadership, 164–7
Herzl, Theodor, 15, 80
Heseltine, Michael, 135, 199
Hildebrand, Peter, 160, 161
Hitler, Adolf, 11, 17, 32, 80, 108, 137
Hogg, Quintin, 55
Hoggart, Simon, 212–13
Home Office Advisory Committee-

on the Penal System, 192,
194–5
Homeostasis, 177–8
Homogamy, 106–7, 108, 109,
121–2
Homosexual rivalry, 200, 201,
204–6
Hooson, Emlyn, 4
Horner, Arthur, 103
Howard, Michael, 192–3, 196,
199
Hutton, Will, 186, 208
Hysterical personality, the, 155,
156

'In Bloom', 136
Independent, 133
Independent on Sunday, 105
In Place of Strife, 102
In Utero, 137
Institute for Scientific Treatment
of Delinquency, 173–4
In vitro research, 7
Israel, 40

Jagger, Mick, 57, 69, 127, 130,
131, 132, 133
Jenkins, Roy, 24, 76, 204–5
Johnson, Joy, 209–10
Johnson, Samuel, 67
Jones, Alec, 53
Jones, Ernest, 111–12
Jung, Carl, 154

Kaletsky, Anatole, 104, 188, 210
Khomeini, Ayatollah, 123
King, Anthony, 10
King, Martin Luther, 40
Kinks, The, 131
Kinnock, Neil, 6, 154
Kohut, Heinz, 72

Krohn, Alan, 156

Labour Co-ordinating Com-
mittee, 120
Labour Party, The, 11, 12; and
1994 leadership election, 9–10;
and rivalry between Bevan and
Gaitskell, 18, 19, 25; and
H-bomb debate, 23; the
mother-orientated Old Labour
movement, 31, 41, 85; and
self-acclaimed modernisation,
41–2, 44, 62; Blair's designs
on, 62, 178–9; the federal
nature of, 91–2; and the
antagonism between labour
and capitalism, 102–3; the
1995 Conference of, 104,
107–8, 146; and Cherie Blair,
120; influence of the 'New
Democrats' within, 126–7; and
religion, 144–5; and
'Blurrism', 181; and Blair's
'deadwood', 208–9, 214–15;
Blair's hijacking of, 208–15; *see
also* Clause Four, *Road to the
Manifesto*
Langdon, Julia, 200, 202
Language, 43, 209–10; and
populism, 44; and euphemism,
44–5
Lansbury, George, 82
Laski, Harold, 78
Laslett, Peter, 153
Lawson, Alvin, 137–8, 140–41
Lawson, Nigel, 188
Leadership: outsider and insider
leaders, 80; traumatised, 122,
123; narcissistic, 124–5
Lee, Jennie, 36

Le Monde, 48
Live With Me, 131
Lloyd George, David, 43, 48, 80
Love objects, 124
Lynn, Vera, 131, 132
Lynton, Jimmy *see* Parsons, Charles

Macmillan, Harold, 199, 212
Macmurray, John, 92–9, 101, 113, 127, 130, 176, 206
Major, John, 11, 31, 49, 60
Mandela, Nelson, 11, 17, 40
Mandelson, Peter, 72, 154, 181, 202; dowry scheme of, 157–9
Marx, Karl, 211
Matrimonial and Family Proceedings Bill, The, 53, 55, 58, 59, 61
Maxwell, Robert, 203, 204
Mellor, David, 203
Mirror-gazing, 72
Mitterrand, François, 48
Monmouthshire, 36
Moore, Suzanne, 132, 133
MORI polls, 9, 10
Morris, Bill, 65
Morris, William, 66
Morrison, Herbert, 72–4
Mosley, Oswald, 148
Mothership Connection, 137
Mother's Milk, 137
Mourning-liberation process, 162–3
Murdoch, Rupert, 178
Mussolini, Benito, 157

Narcissism, 50, 69–70, 71, 72, 78, 88, 119, 120, 163; and love objects, 124; and youth, 153; and the mother, 175–6, 184
National Health Service, 29, 31, 197
Nazi Germany, 146, 148, 149, 150, 159
Nevermind, 136–7
'New Democrats', the, 126, 127, 128
New Party, the, 148–9
New Statesman, 99
News of the World, 130
Nirvana, 134, 136–7
Nixon, Richard, 15

Oasis, 134
Observer, 62, 154, 178, 181–2, 197–8
Oedipal rites of passage, 33, 34, 182–3, 184
Oedipal rivalries, 113
Oral deprivation, 75, 76
Outsiders, 79, 80, 81, 82–3, 84–6
Owen, David, 118
Oxford Union, 4–5, 90
Oxford University, 84, 89, 90, 96, 97

Palingenesis, 146–7, 148, 149, 154, 158, 163, 172, 176
Panell, Charles, 25
Parris, Matthew, 64–5, 66, 67
Parsons, Charles, 113, 114, 115, 118
'Peace at Home', 121
Pearl Jam, 139
Perversion, 167–8, 169–71; its core complex, 171–2; and aggression, 172–4, 175–6; the Marquis de Sade on, 179–81

Pétain, Henri Philippe, 157
Peter Pan syndrome, the, 133, 134
Peyre, Henri, 11
Philby, Kim, 86
Picture of Dorian Gray, The, 153
Pollock, George, 162–3
Pontypool, 19
Portillo, Michael, 199
P.O.V., 140
Powell, Enoch, 7
Prescott, John, 126, 135
Press, Joy, 134–5, 137
Private Member, 61
'Prodigal Son', 141
Prospect, 208

Q, 134, 142

Raven, Charlotte, 154–5
Reagan, Ronald, 67
Redwood, John, 199
Refuge, 121
Renewal and rebirth, myth of, 145–6, 147; and fascism, 148–9; and the nation and family, 157–9
Rentoul, John, 115, 126–7
Reynolds, Simon, 134–5, 137
Richard, Cliff, 133
Road to the Manifesto, 211, 212–13
Robespierre, Maximilien François Marie Isidore de, 123
Rock music: and return to the womb, 136–8; and pre-natal memories, 138–9, 140; and symbolism, 139; and rebirth imagery 140–41
Rock rebels, 134–5

Rodgers, Lord, 24
Rolling Stones, The, 131, 133, 135, 141
Rowntree Foundation, 152

Sartre, Jean-Paul, 134–5
Scargill, Arthur, 103
Schiller, Johann Christoph Friedrich von, 170
Scottish Young Communist League, 79
SDP, 120
Sex Pistols, The, 134
Sibling rivalry, 78–9; and Blair, 150; and politicians, 200–201
Silverman, Sidney, 189
Simpson, Mark, 133, 134
Smashing Pumpkins, 140–41
Smith, John, 3–11; perfectionism of, 5–6; and the 'malady of the ideal', 6, 8–9; his principles, 6–8; his family roots, 7
Smith, Logan Pearsall, 76
Smith, Professor Dai, 30
Social Democrats *see* SDP
Society and community, 94–6
Solitude, 74–5
Sopel, Jon, 83, 88, 89, 113–14
Soskice, Frank, 24
Southern, Sir Richard, 97
Sowing the Seeds of Love, 137
Stakeholder Society, the, 104–5
Stalin, Joseph, 108
State We're In, The, 186
Steiner, Riccardo, 60
Stephenson, Phoebe, 58
Stooges, The, 134
Strachey, John, 39, 45
Stroll On, 119
Sun, 99, 178

Sunday Times, 203

Tavistock, Clinic, 160
Taylor, A J P, 122
Tebbit, Norman, 80
Television, 48, 49, 209; and
  mirror-gazing, 72
Thatcher, Margaret, 11, 31, 48,
  50, 57, 58, 125, 179, 211
Theatricality, 64, 66, 67–8
Thomas, George *see* Tonypandy,
  Viscount
Thomson, Peter, 92, 206–7
Till Death Us Do Part, 119
Times, The, 60, 64, 104–5, 181,
  202, 207
Toad the Wet Sprocket, 139
Tocqueville, Alexis Charles Henri
  Clérel de, 44
Today, 49
Tonypandy, Viscount, 18, 144
Totem and Taboo, 114–15
Totemism, 22–3
Townsend, Peter, 105
Transport and General Workers'
  Union, 65, 91–2
Treasury, The, 187–8

Trotsky, Leon, 80, 214–15
Tse-tung, Mao, 155
TUC Conference (1995), 101–2,
  103–4

Ugly Rumours, The, 131
Universal community, 98

Walk on the Ocean, 139
Weber, Max, 16–17, 109
Welfare State, 31, 149, 197
Wellington, Duke of, 161
Wilde, Oscar, 153
Williams, Shirley, 120
Wilson, Harold, 37, 38, 62, 63,
  64, 102, 144; and false consen-
  sus, 61; garrulousness of,
  75–6; and his inner circle, 207
Wilson, Mary, 119
Winnicott, Donald, 74, 100–101
Wotan, My Enemy, 131–2

Young, Hugo, 57–8, 102, 179
'Yours', 132

Zilboorg, Gregory, 192